Interwoven Wild:

An Ecologist Loose In the Garden

Interwoven Wild:

An Ecologist Loose In the Garden

Don Gayton

thistledown press

Library and Archives Canada Cataloguing in Publication

Gayton, Don, 1946-
Interwoven wild : an ecologist loose in the garden / Don Gayton.

ISBN 978-1-897235-35-5

1. Garden ecology. 2. Gardens in art. 3. Gardens in literature.
4. Landscape in art. I. Title.

SB450.97.G39 2007   77.5'54   C2007-904530-8

Cover photo by Don Gayton
Cover and book design by Jackie Forrie
Printed and bound in Canada

Thistledown Press Ltd.
633 Main Street
Saskatoon, Saskatchewan, S7H 0J8
www.thistledownpress.com

 Canada Council Conseil des Arts
for the Arts du Canada

 Canadian Patrimoine
Heritage canadien

Thistledown Press gratefully acknowledges the financial assistance of
the Canada Council for the Arts, the Saskatchewan Arts Board, and
the Government of Canada through the Book Publishing Industry
Development Program for its publishing program.

For Percy Wright
In Memory

Contents

Split Eden   9

Working the Saprophytes   21

Honour the Edge   34

Weeds "R" Us   47

The Movement of Plants   59

The Rhythm of Trees   74

The Art of the Yard   81

Toad Hall   90

Che Among the Cotoneasters   96

The Climate of the Kettle   112

Consider the Lilacs   124

Categories and Calyces   133

Here if Anywhere   141

Gardening Dry   152

A Place to Work Things Out   164

The trees were interwoven wild,
And spread their boughs enough about
To keep both sheep and shepherd out,
But not a happy child.

— from "The Deserted Garden"
Elizabeth Barrett Browning (1806-1861)

SPLIT EDEN

THE UNIVERSE IS probably circular and may even be doughnut-shaped, like my yard. The dog and I patrol our suburban doughnut in a clockwise fashion, looking for dandelions. I honestly don't mind dandelions, even the massive, double-muscled kind that thrive in the mild climate of this mountain town. In fact I admire dandelion ecology. I don't hunt them for the sake of neighborly peer pressure; I do it for the pleasure of being in the yard. And I do it for my dog.

Spud is a disreputable longhaired dachshund, who looks like an Irish setter might if it were left in the dryer too long. His registration papers describe him dubiously as "pet quality." The squat, muscular and persistent breed was developed in medieval Europe for pursuing badgers and other fossorial animals, but Spud has strayed dramatically from the breed's mandate, since he hunts dandelions. I honestly can't think of any similarity between badgers and the universal lawn weed, except that both are very hard to get out of the ground. Spud doesn't actually hunt dandelions on his own, at least not yet; he helps me hunt them. When I take the dandelion fork from its place by the front door Spud becomes intensely excited, in much the same way a legitimate hunting dog would react when his master gets out the shotgun. Once I am holding the fork Spud forbids any delays or distractions. Chatting with a neighbour or pinching back a rose is met with a series of stern barks, surprisingly loud and baritone from such a small dog.

I call our suburban doughnut a garden, not a yard, because *garden* is one of the most complex and multilayered words in the entire English language. Just thinking of the modifiers of the term — from alpine to zucchini — dazzles me. And the unmodified terms *garden* or *gardening* have a pleasant ambiguity about them, since they refer to growing plants for food as well as for ornament. I like that ambiguity, because what I do in my yard is an imprecise mixture of landscaping, gardening for food, and the cultivation of ornamentals, together with all the accompanying romance, philosophy and weeding.

Our doughnut-shaped universe slopes downward in a northerly direction, a terrible aspect for gardening. But there is plenty of grey granite rock to be had locally, so for years now I have been excavating and building stone retaining walls, creating little level terraces in between. The rock walls add a motif to the landscaping that I call Unintentional Inca. The level terraces hold small lawns and garden beds, where an eclectic mix of introduced and native plants co-exist with the dandelions.

Rock walls and terraces imply pathways, something I hadn't considered at the beginning of the terracing project. So I found a source of local flagstone from the mountains above town that I could build the pathways with. The salmon-coloured flagstone shapes were irregular, so they went together as a kind of ill-fitting mosaic, with spaces in between and more spaces where they met the rock walls. Landscaping manuals say the proper way to lay a stone walk is on top of a four-inch bed of coarse sand or crushed gravel, which suppresses any vegetation that might spring up in the interstices. I considered the proper method for a while, before I bedded my stones right directly into the dirt. I wasn't sure what might grow in the spaces between the flagstones, but I had hopes for a demure moss cover, elegant but able to withstand human and canine foot traffic. In a few spots, that was indeed what I got. In other spots though, pineapple weed grew up between the cracks. And rank grass in others. And clover in a few. But it was right here, in the cracks of my new walkway, that the garden offered me a revelation, an interstitial insight, if you will.

As the walk winds around to the north side of the house, it passes through a damp and perennially shady spot. Here, the cracks between the flagstones cycled quickly from moss to Kentucky bluegrass. Along the edge, where the pathway met the rock wall, some low ferns appeared, unbidden. The vegetation was obviously following a sequential plan, but it wasn't mine. By fall, this part of the walkway had grown rank with the season's dross of dead ferns and grass, so I got out the grass rake to clean it off. The pile grew steadily as I worked, and the scrape of metal tines against granite created a harsh but satisfying rhythm. Raking gives ample room to think, and I was drifting along nicely when the tines caught on something, and I bent down to look. There, hidden in the leaf litter, was a scrappy young seedling of western red cedar, about six inches high. Its scale-like leaves were so shiny they might have been recently polished. Cedar is common to these mountain ecosystems, and perhaps represents their highest expression. The seed of cedar is light and fluffy, so this would be the windblown progeny of one of several mature trees in the neighbourhood.

Ecological succession was happening right in the northeast corner in my very own yard. Spud was totally unimpressed, but I was both surprised and intrigued.

I am an ecologist, and succession is a concept that lies at the beating heart of my chosen profession. Ecosystem is a collection of interrelated organisms, rooted in a landscape. Ecosystem is a noun, but succession is the fundamental and fascinating verb in the grammar of ecology, describing how a community of organisms changes in response to time, climate and disturbance. For decades, I had been practising my ecology by going away from home, enmeshing myself in some distant native grassland or alpine forest. I was an ecological farfarer, compelled to learn landscapes and their intricate successional processes in obscure parts of this continent. But here, literally on my own doorstep, was a fine example of succession, a cycling from moss to grass to fern to cedar. In their accumulated wisdom, these plants took the measure of my contrived flagstone environment and created life, habitat, niche, and community. And they performed an elegant, partnered dance among themselves to move that community forward. Forward in stature, in complexity, in interrelation, in succession. I looked up from the little cedar seedling and surveyed the lilac hedge, the rose garden and the nearby lawn in a new light. My own humble and contrived garden, the very ground that I knew best and visited most often, could also be a fertile field for ecological observation. Not only that, the yard also offered a pleasant laboratory in which to observe the natural against the artificial — how my human creations meshed or clashed with those of nature. And how cultural perceptions would put their own curious spin on the whole endeavor. Gardens can act as training wheels for ecologists, and nature in turn can tutor the landscaper.

Biologists of literary inclination seem always to be drawn to evolution. They sense a high concept, rife with conflict, an observational frame they can place around all events. I myself am much more attracted to a lesser mystery. Succession is evolution's poor, but far more entertaining cousin. It's not nearly as exalted, but way more fun. The timescale of evolution is typically marked in eons, so we can only engage it through forensics. But succession happens at the time scale of human generations; if you're patient, you can see it happen. And once in a while it happens in a season, in between grey granite and salmon flagstone.

Revelation is a pretty grand and biblical word. I would use a diminutive form to describe my little cedar event, but the dictionary doesn't offer me one. So I'll stick with revelation — the astonishing disclosure, the lifting of the veil, the momentary surprise that triggers a slight but permanent shift in consciousness. There is sweet irony in the fact that it took years of travel before I realized my profession could be practiced at home.

Much of what I need to know, as an ecologist and as a man, I can learn in the garden. I've lived with scientific ecology, and read many tomes on deep ecology. Now I'm content to work on a canine-friendly, street-level hybrid, which I call shallow ecology.

Dogs are wonderful touchstones, rudely interrupting philosophical vagaries with their urgent need to chase something. I do my dandelion weeding on hands and knees, which puts me close to my dog's level. So intent is Spud on capture that he often stands directly over the plant I am about to dig out, alert to any sign of movement. This dog's clearance off the ground is such that I have to distract him momentarily while I use the digging fork to lever the dandelion out of the soil. The payoff comes when I flip the severed weed high into the suburban sky. With a twisting, graceful leap, my overstuffed, furry sausage snags the weed in midair, brings it to ground, and administers the *coup de grace* in the form of a vigorous headshake. This is followed by a quick, efficient dismemberment, and then he drops the corpse, intent on the next prey. Size does matter with this dog; he much prefers the heavier dandelions with flowers the size of tennis balls and roots like turnips.

Now this canine behaviour seems like a far cry from the skillset required to bring down (bring up?) a badger in the wild, but perhaps Spud's idiosyncrasy matches the skewed and eclectic way that I approach gardens and ecosystems. My transit is along a continuum that starts with the habitat of the house, moves outward to the fabricated ecologies of yard and garden, passes through disturbed ground and vacant lot, dawdles through landscape architecture, parks, agriculture, forests and grasslands, reaches all the way out to embrace classical ecosystems in our remaining shards of actual wilderness, and then cycles back again. I transplant ideas germinated in garden beds out into nature, to see how they do, and sometimes I bring a fragile wild concept back to my yard. My brand of ecology is occasionally angry, because of our heedless disrespect for nature, but indiscriminate to the point that it accepts a good portion of our humanity.

Even before I step out my front door I am enveloped in intriguing ecological processes and ideas. The ring-porous structure of our bookshelf of red oak. The treasured volumes upon it — a heady mixture of wood pulp and good writing. The absurdly complex nitrogen cycle of the tropical fish aquarium next to the bookshelf. The way we choose to organize our homes into living room, bedroom, kitchen. More and more I realize the ecology I used to practice only in grasslands and forests has a far greater reach. This humble new science telescopes in many directions, and has a kind of magic glue that can bind culture, science and economics together. The last century may have belonged to the physicists, but this next one may well belong to a ragtag bunch of ecologists.

The front door is a constant in human dwellings, and yet its diversity of form and style rivals the fantastical starfishes. We ask the door to perform the contradictory duties of separation, ostentation, security, and welcome. This is a difficult enough task, but we also ask the doorway to provide a soft transition from outside to inside, from the outdoor, biophysical world to the world of human domesticity, and we do that with plantings around the house entrance. An arbour over the door, a trellis beside it, or an adjacent bed of roses mixed with daffodils. Or the traditional pyramidal cedars planted on either side, like Beefeater sentries. One can almost envision that ancestral time when our door was the mouth of the family cave, and we brushed aside the hanging vine as we entered.

I chose English ivy to mediate my own front door nature-to-culture transition. This turned out to be serious mistake. Being recently delivered from the rigours of fifteen years living in a Canadian prairie climate, I was eager to take advantage of British Columbia's famous mildness by planting things that would stay green and succulent all winter. Ivy seemed the perfect choice to soften the doorway and give the house that settled, English countryside look. Within three seasons, the new ivy had indeed wreathed our front door with its lush, dark green leaves. Then I discovered holdfasts, which are ivy's equivalent of crazy glue, only stronger. By year six, wrist-thick vines were coiling underneath the molding, loosening the mullions, and peeling back the transom. Looking further, I discovered all the new ivy growth was taking place *underneath* my vinyl siding. English ivy had turned incubus; it was taking over the house. I had a long discussion about the ivy with my wife Judy, who accepts all plants and animals unconditionally, without judgment, except for rattlesnakes. She is even dubious about the morality of pruning. After showing Judy the domestic carnage and gaining her reluctant permission to euthanize, I sliced through the knotted and muscular ivy stems right at ground level, and waited. After a full month the leaves finally began to wilt, and I tore the entire monstrosity off the house. Years later I can still see ivy's imprint on the siding. The holdfasts are permanent, almost like claw marks. A colleague told me about a similar ivy experience; mysterious trippings of their home alarm system were eventually traced to ivy tendrils doing break-and-enters through the window transoms.

I was very familiar with the ecological concept of invasiveness, but now it had arrived at my front door. My attempt at transition aesthetics had become a home invasion. I went back to trite but well-mannered daffodils.

Beyond our south-facing front door are the garden beds, where my constructed ecologies and frivolities are played out. Here, delicate native glacier lilies coexist with supermarket daisies. A bluebunch wheatgrass from Rocky Mountain grasslands competes for space with a flowering almond from China. A fussy native camas, which took years to establish, grows hard by a dirt-common forsythia. Food plants are mingled with ornamentals, herbs with shrubs, and conifers with broadleaves. The whole yard has a kind of comfortably alien look about it. Then there is the gigantic rhubarb plant, happily occupying a wet spot in the back garden, boldly advertising its ornamental, nutritional, pharmaceutical, allegorical and sexual wares. Its massive floral structure is like some rude phallic obscenity. No wonder early herbalists were so in awe of plants like the rhubarb; its root could cure "wamblings of the gut," its stems were delicious, and its leaves would kill you. This tough plant is also an indicator of failed domestic settlement, since a thriving bull rhubarb plant is often the last vestige of abandoned homesteads throughout the rural West.

The only care my rhubarb gets is when I pull the odd pale and starving weed from underneath its broad canopy. Independent, contradictory and multilayered, this plant is the flagship of my yard. If our house were a grand manor, which it is definitely not, the heraldic escutcheon would have a rhubarb salient on the dexter side, and a dachshund rampant on the sinister.

A 40 x 100 foot suburban house lot hardly qualifies as an ecosystem, created or not, but then we scientists are hard pressed to define ecosystems even in larger and undisturbed nature. My landscaping and garden beds might be called microecosystems in training. I used to worry that this eclectic style of landscaping would reveal my eccentricities to the neighbours, who might see me as a kind of low-rent mad king, planting labyrinthine hedges and hauling in Greek statuary. But time and succession are on my side; as the terraces settle in and the rocks, weather and plants mature, they begin to look as if they had always been there. This allows me to shift blame for the idiosyncracy on to the Original Property Owner.

My garden and yard are actually not at all distinctive. Their only conceit is that I started them from scratch — from a featureless lawn, one mountain ash tree, one massive balsam fir, and an overgrown lilac hedge. I have had the unique privilege of planning, executing and then living with the results of my own landscaping decisions. I confess to being a very ordinary gardener. I put in plants that are supposed to attract butterflies, and all I get are cabbage loopers. But I seem destined to learn from dozens of instructive mistakes.

With ecosystems come food chains, one of which is unfolding in my yard. It starts with crows, which are very bright and have way too much free time on their hands. The crows in my neighbourhood have developed a taste for the black walnut, a tree native to eastern North America but introduced in the West as an ornamental. The crows bring the nuts from nearby trees to the top of a strategically placed power pole in our front yard, which leans over the steps of the front walk. Most of the walnuts crack on the flagstones when the crows drop them, giving them access to the nutmeat inside, but a few do not. Those that don't tend to bounce into the street, which heads downhill at a twelve-percent grade. Gathering speed and momentum, the walnuts bounce erratically on the rough pavement of this mountain town. The crows generally do their walnut work early in the morning, as my late-rising dachshund would certainly interfere with their operations, but early morning is also prime time for neighbourhood cats, which are busy preying on the native songbirds. I think it is the eccentric and unpredictable motion of the uncracked, rolling walnuts that galvanize the cats. Upon seeing a fleeing walnut, they instantly drop their maimed chickadees and bolt into the street, thus putting themselves at risk of the guy in the Ford F-350 who is late for the early shift at the sawmill.

The crows (omnivorous scavengers) then happily switch from walnuts (primary producers) to squashed cats (apex predators). So the crow-walnut-cat-songbird-truck-crow cycle, however brutal and bizarre it may be, has now become a local food chain of sorts, and food chains are fundamental to every ecosystem, even suburban ones.

As I slowly develop my doughnut micro-ecosystem, I am sure to be following some deeply laid unconscious pattern. Like a bird weaving leaves and twigs into a nest, I do not need to be told what to do. The patiently built rock walls, the perennial beds and the small lawns are all the hazy realization of some deep cultural template, overlain with personal idiosyncracy. Even if I were influenced by furtive readings of gardening magazines at newsstands, which of course I am not, I would still be working from someone else's interpretation of a deep blueprint. I make no apologies if the basic gardening pattern I follow harkens to the English country estate, or farther back to the hills of Arcadia, or perhaps all the way to ancient Babylon. Humans have always had a difficult relationship with nature, but early on in our development we discovered a valuable mediator, in the patterns of our gardens.

Most commercial landscaping is a vile form of tokenism, but true landscaping is almost always in the service of the split Eden;

the cultivated, and the wild. We like having shaped and subservient plantings right alongside the unplanned and unkempt ones. Letting nature impose its own arrangement is somehow as attractive to us as arranging it ourselves. Oddly, this contradictory duality — the taking hold and the letting go — courses well beyond yard and garden into our very understanding of nature.

Clockwise from the house's front door we (the dog and I) reach the grape arbour, and next to it, the garden shed. Beyond the shed is a narrow space between my house and the neighbour's, which I am developing as a domestic proxy for a shady forest glen. At its other end, the glen opens up to a pocket-sized backyard. Beyond that we each the lower end of the sloping doughnut, which is bounded by an alley. Alleys are the ragged edges of suburban yard ecosystems. They form the Quiet Back, where neglect is the dominant ecological force, witnessed by rank grass, spent cars that with only a few hundred dollars could be running again, and geriatric fences leaning at crazy angles. Spud and I have designated our back area as a dandelion preserve; the season is permanently closed here.

Once, I planted a hop vine on my own back alley fence. The hop, which is a European introduction, has a tangy smell that always makes me think of pubs in the afternoon. This planting was yet another mistake. Now, years later, I am responsible for the surging vines that strangle and pull down alley fences of every neighbour on the block. But fortunately ecology has come to my rescue. This time it is the human ecology of benign neglect. No one has noticed the hops.

WORKING THE SAPROPHYTES

ECOLOGY REPLICATES A deep cycle of going away, and of coming back. Of going away to the experiences of the field and then coming back to the abstraction of ideas. Of observing plants and animals, and then distilling those observations into hunches and theories. One of the real advantages of doing ecology in the garden is that it saves a long road trip. Primary observations can be made right in one's front yard, and the secondary abstraction and synthesis can be done there too. You don't even need to go inside. I do a lot of the thoughtful part of the ecological cycle while working my compost bin.

At one time, my idea of composting was to put dead stuff into a pile and leave it out back. I have since come to see the compost bin more as a family pet — a living organism that offers pleasure, but which also needs care and attention, and the occasional scratch behind the ears. To reflect my current attitude, I moved the compost pile from its former place of shame next to the garbage can in the alley, to a prominent location in the front yard. And I built a bin for it, a spacious 2-holer, using waste cedar slabs from the local sawmill. The slabs are nailed on bark side out, and as they weather, the bark peels off gradually, hanging down in ropy and interesting patterns. One of the bin's corner posts is tall, and serves as an attachment point for a hammock. The other end of the hammock attaches to the lichen-covered trunk of the inherited mountain ash tree. Like the homeowner who puts a piece of modern sculpture in the living room, I am making a bold statement by putting my bin in the front yard. The actual meaning of my compost statement is not too clear, but then that is true of a lot of sculpture as well.

As I built the bin, I did experience some performance anxiety. Ecologists are supposed to learn composting shortly after they master tying shoelaces. I could explain the formulas all right, but knew nothing about the actual practice. What if a neighbour came over and pointed out some rookie error? So the first season I started slowly and discreetly, but by midsummer I realized just how forgiving composting really is. Mix a few ingredients in a pile, add a bit of water, and stir occasionally. A delightful little bestiary of worms, bugs, fungi and bacteria will appear as if by magic. The middle of a working compost pile is a veritable biological kingdom.

With my formal bin, I've tried to move beyond haphazard additions. If I have a whole raft of grapevine clippings, for example, I don't throw them all into the bin at once. Half gets set aside until a layer of something else can go in between. Nobody likes a monotonous diet, not even bacteria. So broccoli stem bases get mixed with straw from the floor of the rabbit's cage, coffee grounds with fruit tree prunings, and so on. Such are the pleasant rituals of compost.

Woody stems, twigs and corncobs are my biggest challenge; they thumb their noses at the decomposing abilities of my highly skilled compost cadre of worms, bugs and microbes.

When I realized I was seeing the same twigs and stems cycling from bin to garden and back to the bin again unscathed, I knew it was time for drastic action. I now cut these items into small pieces using a pair of sharp pruning shears. (I should perhaps call them "secateurs," thus providing a semantic signal that I am actually a serious gardening professional.) So it is during these long cutting sessions in front of the compost bin that I contemplate the pleasant mysteries of shallow ecology.

I am very conscious of compost odours, which would simultaneously repel neighbours and attract local black bears. Whenever I put a bunch of wet, juicy kitchen stuff into the bin, I always mix dry, stemmy stuff in along with it, to maintain the sweet and subtle odour. Even in fall time, when a lot of unused fruit goes into my bin, the smell never goes septic. A friend suggested that I consider wearing a lab coat when I work my compost. Now that would certainly be overkill, but I have become inordinately proud of the rich black stuff that we (the bugs and I) produce. One of my many summer garden pleasures is to sprawl in my hammock, doing nothing, while my compost bugs work their skinny little asses off.

I do look forward to the summer sweet corn season, partly because I love corn on the cob, and partly because of the husks, which I found to be wonderful compost material that breaks down almost immediately. Husks are the biological opposite of cobs, which are as durable as mahogany. Shortly after I discovered the beauty of cornhusks, the local grocery store set up a plastic garbage bin next to their sweet corn display, allowing customers to shuck their corn right on the spot. This allowed me to periodically trundle off with the contents of the bin, much to the delight of the store manager. Surely the gods of recycling had a hand in this fortunate circumstance.

Gardening has now gone upscale to the point that you can pay fifty dollars for a personalized weeding cushion, so I am surprised no one has started marketing boutique compost. The promotional material for such an upscale product might go something like this. "Sideyard, 1999. Redolent of herbs and humus, Sideyard is carefully aged in natural cedar and turned by hand, using cold-rolled, ungalvanized pitchforks. You will be satisfied by the calcium-rich mellowness, and agreeably surprised by the robustness of its red wigglers."

A fundamental responsibility of every gardener — and perhaps non-gardeners as well — is the enhancement of the soil. One might even think of good soil as the real product of landscaping and gardening; the plants are almost secondary. Good soil means good plants. The essence of a soil is *not* its proportion of sand, silt and clay; rather it is the amount of organic matter it contains. Organic matter, composed of stable carbon compounds called humic acids, are the ones that give soil its wonderful rotting-log smell. This is the primeval odour of fructification, of compost, of succession. To exceed ten percent organic matter in one's garden soil is to arrive at a highly evolved karmic state.

Composting consists of transplanting a soil-based process out of its normal environment, concentrating it, accelerating it, and then dispersing the end product back to the soil. It is remarkable how such a wide variety of ingredients, a multitude of secret family compost recipes and rigorous biodynamic prescriptions all produce the same rich, dark product — the colour and texture of German chocolate cake. As I add a load of fresh plant material to the compost bin, I usually scatter a thin layer of garden soil on top, just to kick-start the breakdown process. When I open up a finished bin, it always looks like I've added way too much soil, but the great mass of fine dark particles is actually organic matter, broken down to the size and texture of soil.

A composting process is writ large across the Canadian and American prairies, which originally possessed the highest organic matter content of any upland soils on the planet. The architects of that organic matter were the humble bunchgrasses, native perennials whose great masses of deeply probing, short-lived roots broke down to produce the dark, pH-neutral and incredibly productive soils of the prairies. Bunchgrasses, together with the massive herds of ruminant bison that recycled them, and the ever-willing soil fauna, functioned like a continental-scale compost bin, creating the wonderful dark-coloured soils we know as chernozems. But cultivation and humus accumulation are fundamentally incompatible; with prairie grain farming, we eliminate the perennials and the ruminants, substitute annual plants with far smaller root systems, and remove most of the crop biomass instead of returning it to the land. And several times a year we stir the soil, each time exposing more humus to bacterial breakdown. Ecology is full of ironies: the same soil fauna that produce humus can also break it down, under the right conditions.

In a classic case of not being content with harvesting the annual interest, a hundred years of prairie agriculture has severely depleted nature's organic matter capital, a depletion no amount of fertilization can fix. There is a lesson here for us gardeners.

In my garden, I practice a strange micro-variant of agriculture. When I weed, I stir the soil extensively; some of my plants are annuals, and I remove part of each year's crop. But there is a significant difference between agriculture and my garden, which is best explained by a model.

Modelling — building mathematical analogues of natural systems — is one of the abstract sporting grounds some ecologists like to play on. Models provide a different perspective on ecosystems, one that is built up from numerical inputs, outputs and relationships. Models tend to emphasize processes, and relationships. By assigning numbers to fundamental concepts like energy or carbon allocation, the ecologist is forced to become explicit about what can be well-formed yet fuzzy assumptions. Models sometimes generate surprising results. In the early heydays of modelling, I worked with a scientist who was attempting to model the flow of biomass through a native prairie. He developed estimates of every conceivable factor, from plant growth to insectivory to soil respiration, and fed them into an early mainframe computer large enough to fill a house trailer. Then he and his colleagues turned the model on and let it run. Very quickly the scientists realized they had incorrectly estimated a key parameter, since their virtual prairie had become covered with a waist-deep layer of virtual grasshopper poop.

My own garden model is a series of boxes and connecting lines; it stops just short of the mathematical part. The primary source box in my garden model is Total Annual Yard Biomass Production. Directional arrows radiate from that first big box to other secondary "sink" boxes. The biggest of this second tier of boxes is Unharvested Growth, the live and dead perennial stuff that stays in the garden. Next is Harvested For Compost, and underneath them a smaller sink box called Harvested For Food. A little side source box called Kitchen Waste is joined to Harvested for Compost by another arrow. Two very small source boxes labelled Dryer Lint and Wine Corks also fed into Harvested for Compost, until I discovered these two items to be even more durable than twigs and corncobs. The large size of the Harvested for Compost box is what sets my garden model apart from most of modern agriculture, which recycles very little. Hidden inside this box are magical biological processes that turn all those raw materials into compost. The final arrow leaving the Compost box is called Biomass Return To The Garden, which in turn enhances the Total Annual Biomass Production box. Smaller side flows can also be factored in to the model, such as Authorized Dog Droppings and Illicit Cat Input.

Fortunately, I don't spend a lot of time modelling.

I do entertain a certain amount of guilt about my garden annuals. When I pull out a tomato plant or a geranium at the end of the season and look at its skimpy, undernourished root system, I think, "you just took and took, and you didn't put anything back." So my composting is partly to atone for the sins of growing some horticultural and ornamental annuals in amongst the perennials. With the exception of the legumes, annuals are ecological takers, expending very little in the development of root systems. From a soil organic matter point of view, the ideal garden would be composed of magnificent fibrous-rooted and tap-rooted perennials mixed with occasional shrubs and trees, whose roots can explore deep into the subsoil. The garden's topsoil would rarely be disturbed by shovel or hoe, and the patient process of natural humus production would go on simultaneously underground, as roots decompose, and at the soil surface, as dead plant matter is slowly broken down and pulled into the soil. Every few years there would be a fire or a grazing event, to rejuvenate things. In other words, the ideal garden would be a savanna.

Several years ago it became fashionable to put small indoor composters in the coffee rooms of government offices. Staff would dump their orange peels and apple cores into it, and some very junior official actually came around to inoculate all the composters with red wiggler worms. It takes a lot of orange peels and coffee grounds to make much compost, but after some years of slow accretion, these coffee-room bins would finally be full of beautiful, fine-textured stuff, ready to use and devoid of the usual woody stalks and twigs. The ugly question of ownership then arose; who should get the compost, or should each employee get two handfuls? Retirement gifts became the obvious solution, accompanied with lots of har-hars about how much time the retiree would now have to garden.

I got to know the Minister of Health in a previous government; he once confided in me that, as a rural kind of guy, one of the greatest personal legacies of his term in office was the full compost container the office staff gave him when he lost his seat in an election.

Like most suburbanites, I periodically drag bottles, cans and newspapers to the recycling depot; but I never get much personal satisfaction from it. When I arrive at the depot I always get the sensation that I am aiding and abetting some vast economic perpetual-consumption machine, dutifully recycling the Tetrapaks and supermarket flyers that never should have been produced in the first place. Composting, on the other hand, is a true form of recycling, and one of the very few opportunities the suburbanite has to actually give something back to the earth. Composting is also a form of recycling that appeals to my selfish instincts. I never get to see the tangible benefit of recycling my cans and bottles. With composting, I can be ecologically correct and greedy at the same time.

So my compost bin gets great respect, as does the kitchen waste container. This sealed container, which sits on the kitchen counter, gets all the kitchen scraps except for meat, and is emptied into the bin every week or so. The temporary container receives apple cores, carrot tops, broccoli bums, onion skins, banana peels, cat and dog hair, dust bunnies — the bugs love it all. The container is right next to the cutting board, so scraps go right in as vegetables are prepared. In the summer, fruit flies like to get a head start on the biological action, and I have learned how to make the lightning-fast scrap deposits, and then slam the lid back down so the flies stay inside the container.

My family consumes most vegetables with gusto, except for zucchini and eggplant. When I prepare these vegetables, I make generous donations to the kitchen container. On the sensory scale between Being and Nothingness, zucchini and eggplant are pretty far down the list. In fact, a colleague of mine actually won honourable mention in a zucchini recipe competition with the following entry: "take one large, well-formed zucchini, freshly harvested from the garden, dice carefully into one-inch squares, and arrange them neatly in the compost bin."

I believe the kitchen compost container to be an essential item of haute cuisine, like balsamic vinegar and clarified butter. I look forward to the time when I can trade in my cheap plastic container for an elegant stainless steel one, with a tasteful floral design and perhaps a personalized monogram on the front.

In my excitement about composting, I do need to remind myself that compost bins are but a substitute for ruminant livestock, and the ultimate recycling arrangement is a sheep or a cow in every front yard. However, until City bylaws change, I'm stuck with the compost bin.

I live within the sprawling drainage basin of the Columbia, a river that has acted as a vast composter in its own right. Legions of returning salmon once swam the Columbia's two thousand kilometre main stem and unnumbered tributaries in search of their natal spawning grounds. When these spawned-out salmon died, the nutrients contained in their bodies were transferred into the bodies of bears, ospreys, eagles, crows and insects, and thence into the plants and trees that clothe the Columbia basin. Here is another continental-scale composting operation that we have flagrantly disrupted. The multiple impacts on the Columbia salmon, from dams to pollution to overfishing, are gradually starving its interior ecosystems of that precious marine derived fertility.

By bringing nutrients to it from afar, my humble composting bin is a token recognition of the grand salmon cycle that was so crucial to the natural life of the Columbia River basin.

Composting has nudged me toward a seasonal biorhythm. In the winter I don't turn the pile at all, to preserve whatever residual warmth the pile might still contain. In the spring and fall I turn it a few times, but in the heat of summer, I turn it once or twice a week. My cue is the biorhythms of the red wigglers. The faster they thrash around, the more I turn. In August, I am as hyperactive as they are. These unique little worms, easily identifiable by their small size, pointed tails and general excitability, seem to spontaneously appear wherever manure or dead vegetation accumulate. Charles Darwin was the first to identify their role in the formation of "vegetable mould" (the word *compost* hadn't been invented yet) though he had no way of knowing that the wigglers don't actually eat plant material, they eat the corpses of the bacteria that do eat the plant material.

During our mild, wet springs my garden beds perform well, but the hot days of July and August expose my organic matter shortcomings. Areas that have never received compost, and those that have gone several years without, look peaked. The plants are spindly, yellow and always desperate for water. I can soak them thoroughly one day, and see signs of wilt two days later. The soil surface is pale and hard. Hand weeding is not successful because the plant snaps off in the bony ground, leaving some underground part to regenerate. After inspecting one of these deficient garden areas, I go back to the compost bin and turn it again, urging my saprophytic beasties on to greater effort.

Late fall provides a compost bonus in the form of tree leaves and pumpkins. First I rake the leaves into a giant pile and then throw tennis balls into it, because it is such a treat to watch Spud dive into the pile and disappear. After some time he triumphantly reappears, leaf-bedraggled, with the ball in his mouth. Reluctantly, I move the pile to the compost bin, and alternate a layer of leaves with a layer of smashed Hallowe'en pumpkins, which my neighbours are more than happy to get rid of.

Pumpkins are odd vegetables. No one really owns a pumpkin; they kind of belong to the neighbourhood, particularly to young pranksters and old composters.

My lengthy compost-shredding meditations have lately turned to the ecologist Harold Odum. For many of my generation whose first exposure to ecology was through his famous textbook, he is like a shared cultural memory. I picture him standing knee deep in the Florida Everglades, scanning the assembled plants and fish and invertebrates he understood so well. He is balding, wearing wire frame glasses and a clean white shirt, a kind of ecological grandfather figure. Odum's world was reassuring; as ecosystems progressed, there was more internal integration, more mutual reliance between species, and less energy and fewer nutrients were lost from the system. Short-lived species were gradually replaced by long-lived ones. There was a progressive shift in community focus from freewheeling reproduction to sober longevity. Many of the various forms of disturbances would subside. This was Odum's concept of ecological succession, a complex internal formula that gently shepherded each natural community toward its unique climax identity, and provided the blueprints for reconstruction after disturbance. Much of Odum's thinking is now under attack, by the chaos theorists and others, but one of his fundamental principles has stood the test of time: climax or late successional ecosystems all have large accumulations of organic matter.

It occurs to me, that in Odum's terms, my garden is an ecological paradox. It combines high organic matter accumulation along with almost continuous soil disturbance. But the paradox should not surprise me, since gardening is essentially an irrational act.

Arcadia is a mountainous region of Greece, but it has another life as the enduring myth of the wild Eden, of stately trees and statuary interspersed between lofty crags and verdant valleys. This was the domain of Pan, the lush and perfect landscape, mixing elements of the wild and the cultivated. The idea of such a place, as a venue to indulge human pleasure and art, has persisted throughout the centuries. It is entirely predictable that I would want to create something that could be described as Arcadian. Even though it probably never existed in reality, Arcadia is in the back of my mind whenever I landscape. And I am convinced that my route to that mythical destination will be through the compost bin.

Through spring and summer, I fill and turn my two compost bins at random. But come fall, I choose the most advanced bin and continue to turn it, but I don't add anything more to it. The end of season payoff, after months and months of piling, clipping, shredding, kitchen recycling, turning and thinking, is three or four wheelbarrow loads of lovely black compost. The biological reduction process is amazing, since it must be twenty wheelbarrows worth of fresh material that goes into the bin. Stewarding a natural process is a good lesson in patience, and humility.

The official end of my summer gardening season comes when I load up my wheelbarrow with a year's worth of the bin's rich black yield. In distributing the compost, I practice triage, wheeling my barrow into the worst of the garden war zones, meting out shovelfuls of comfort. Someday I hope to reach the settled peace of Arcadia, and that ten percent karmic state.

❧

Honour the Edge

GOING OFF TO an adventure in nature and then coming back home to spin yarns about it, is an ancient cycle that not only created ecology, but probably language as well. The telling definitely improves the adventure, and that impulse to embroider was the putative mother of speech. The place where these adventure stories were first told, and probably the place where humans were born, is the savanna — that ragged hemline between forest and grassland. We associate savanna with Africa, but every continent including ours has them. Savanna reeks of possibility, diversity, invitation, and adventure. We humans are truly edge people, and deep memories of the savanna edge persist today. Psychologists have tested landscape preferences by asking people to choose between photographs of closed forest, of open grassland, and of intermediate, partly treed landscapes. The overwhelming preference is for the interme-diate landscape, the savanna. The one our species was born in. One of my sons had the opportunity to see the savannas of the Amboseli Game Reserve in Kenya. Upon his return, his comment was: "I'd never seen pictures of it before, and really had no preconceptions of the place. But as soon as I got there, I felt as if I had just come home."

Our domestic landscapes are miniature savannas. This was made clear to me one Saturday afternoon when I took a break from the rigours of gardening, and watched a TV nature show on African wildlife. Scattered across the landscape of a Tanzanian game preserve were herds of wonderful beasts — zebras, giraffes, gemsboks and of course, elephants. The hyperactive cameraman finally settled on a long stationary shot of this incredible compendium of animals in a mixed landscape of grass, trees and shrubs. Each class of animals worked different parts of the flora, and carnivores skulked along the flanks. The television images were compelling, but so was my midsummer garden, visible out the window from where I sat. As my gaze wandered between television and garden, a simple and obvious connection fell into place. I had created a savanna. Right down to the feline predator, skulking in the shrubbery.

In landscaping, we work to mental templates. Somewhere, buried deeply underneath the clutter of modern landscape arrangements, from the English country garden to the cover of the latest gardening magazine, lies the Paleolithic savanna template. Specimen trees, clipped grass, pruned shrubs. Intermediate sightlines, plants in groups. That ancient African savanna is all there in our heads, fully complete, and we subconsciously design to it. Our North American savanna, which was found along the moist edges of the prairies, contains the same elements. Most of it is now gone, but memory persists here as well, in the grass swards and stately oaks of city parks and campus commons. With either savanna, the African or the

North American, you could compress it, groom it a bit, add a little irrigation and fertilizer, and it could easily pass for an urban park, golf course or landscaped yard.

Grazers and browsers are part of every savanna ecosystem. In our domestic yard and park savannas, we replace these natural disturbances with mechanical devices. Gone are zebras, antelopes, gemsboks and bison, each manicuring some specific component of the landscape. Enter the fiendish mechanical bestiary that includes riding mowers, hedge trimmers, pruning shears, scythes, orchard saws, weed whackers, bark mulchers and that most unnecessary of all inventions, the leaf blower. We can take a kind of animal comfort in knowing that every time we mow, we are an imperfect replacement for a grazer; when we prune, we are feebly mimicking the browsers.

Modern ecology is an updating of the original cycle of adventure, observation and story. Ecologists make observations in the field, bring them back to the office or laboratory, and spin them into complex and elaborate yarns. Although stories couched in terms like "hypothesis" and "standard deviation" may seem a little dry, I have been to ecological conferences where audiences were breathless, hanging on the speaker's every word. Some of the scientific adventures described can be as compelling as impaling a woolly mammoth with a stone-tipped spear.

These same ecologists are forever casting things in terms of hectares, to give a numerical relationship between organisms and land area. Trees per hectare, total biomass per hectare, red-shafted flickers per hectare, and so on. I guess it was inevitable that I would want to know what fraction of a hectare my garden might be. So I dug into our mortgage documents and found a

True and Certified Copy of the legal lot survey. Figuring the total lot area was easy, but our house is a higgly-piggly collection of corners, doglegs and elbows, so that calculation took some time. Subtracting the house area from the lot area, I arrived at a shockingly small number: my cultivable land base amounts to twenty one-hundredths a hectare, or put more grandiosely, nearly half an acre. Extrapolating to dog density, I got a figure close to five dachshunds per hectare, which is a very sobering thought.

However small my yard domain may be, I am not fully the master of it. The front yard of my little one-fifth of a hectare contains a savanna, in the form of a small oval-shaped lawn of Kentucky bluegrass. It has a rock wall along one long edge, a garden bed along the other, and narrow pathways exiting from either end. I like how the sweeping curve of the lawn mates gracefully with that of the garden bed. This long, sinuous edge is one of my landscaping statements, but it remains a problematic one, since the lawn is forever trying to invade the garden, to sleep with the roses. Determined to put a stop to this, I built a low border of vertically placed flagstones to keep the grass from spilling over into the garden. Not only did that fail to stop the grass, it also prevented me from mowing the edge. Then I turned the flagstones flat, so I could mow right up to the edge. That didn't look as messy, but the grass continued its inexorable march between the stones and into the garden. I pulled up the flagstones, put fine mesh landscape cloth underneath and replaced the flagstones; that slowed the grass down for a season, until it figured out how to produce infinitely small diameter tillers that were able to grow through the mesh. Next I dug a shallow trench between the lawn and the garden bed. The grass promptly grew over the edge and migrated downward, filling in the trench and again groping for the roses. Like molten lava, Kentucky bluegrass was determined to overtake the entire landscape. I bought coils of black plastic lawn edging and staked it in along the vertical face of the trench. Grass grew under and over the edging, and eventually pushed it right over. The whole exercise was beginning to feel like an extended medieval siege. Eventually I gave up on the idea of permanent barriers, and now simply maintain a deep trench along the edge, and rip out the invading grass several times a year. I don't like this arrangement; it is a perpetual test of wills, never resolved. The grass is telling me this razor-sharp lawn-garden boundary is artificial. I can have a clean and narrow edge only for as long as I am prepared to defy ecology and actively maintain it.

In gardens, as in nature, one must honour the edge.

Savanna, and landscaping, are about edge. Much of ecology is about edge. Edge is where you find the resources, the biodiversity, and the tension. The edge defines the centre, as well as the periphery. It turns out that much of urban planning is about edge too, but that's another story. Edge brings ecology and landscape design together, but edge also makes them different. Traditional landscaping typically has hard, narrow and permanent edges, but edges in nature share none of these traits. Our uniform, defined landscaping edges deny natural gradations and the flux of succession. Ecology gets its revenge though, since these built edges rarely stabilize, except by continuous maintenance, or the application of concrete. It is no wonder we are so in love with that material.

We create our landscaping edges with either a slope break, like my embattled trench, or with a physical barrier. In either case, unused soil water accumulates around our edges, encouraging rank growth. And there is the unused (and unmowed) growing space above and to the sides of the edge that the more daring plants will eagerly occupy and thrive in. In my yard, a flat, uninterrupted edge soon becomes no edge at all, as the side with the most aggressive vegetation (read: Kentucky bluegrass) inevitably spills over to the other side. And of course, trimming an edge guarantees further growth along that edge.

Kentucky bluegrass, the alpha invader, has a permanent but shifting role in my life. I retain a vivid early childhood memory of receiving a lovely open-face fried egg sandwich from my mother and taking it out into the back yard to eat it. Intent on the sandwich, I tripped and dropped it, egg-down, into the freshly-mown grass. I was able to quickly reassemble the sandwich in every detail, except for the lurid sprinkles of Kentucky bluegrass cuttings that were stuck all over the immaculate whites and yellows of the egg.

Later on my father taught me how to golf. He would start each round with a stern lecture about the virtues of patience and composure, and by the third hole he would be muttering unspeakably foul curses and viciously smacking the Kentucky bluegrass with his nine iron. Later yet, in my agronomic phase, Kentucky blue became an icon for me, the star performer in irrigated, heavily grazed dairy pastures. Now, in my current protracted ecological phase, it has become a curse, in both my yard and as a major invasive in the native grasslands where I work. I fully expect the grass to transition yet again, and affect my future life in some unexpected way.

I recognize all the difficulties inherent in landscaped edges that are permanent, narrow and defined. Yet I still want them.

Ecosystems have the luxury of making their transitions over kilometres of space; my yard transitions have to happen in a hand's breadth. Terraces and drypointed rock walls are a kind of useful alternative to the maintained edge. They provide more ecological "room" for ragged edges, but over vertical — rather than precious horizontal — space. My first rock walls were built from the random harvest of my excavations — triangular rocks, round rocks, oval rocks, rocks of no definable shape. I soon became more picky, and started scanning local roadsides for the ideal stones for rock walls: rectangular, and about the size of a small suitcase. I soon realized that other landscapers were doing the same thing, and that all the local roadsides were heavily picked over. So as my wall building progressed, the rocks came from further and further afield.

I wish I could say that I created a plan for my rock walls, and that their progression followed a preconceived arrangement. In the garden, I indulge a personality trait that I am barely able to suppress in my working life: I don't plan. The course of a rock wall or the lay of my garden beds evolve directly from the process of building them. If the lowly mollusc doesn't have to think as it lays down the walls of a magnificent spiralled shell, then I too should be granted occasional right to operate as an organism in full sensory touch with my home environment, allowing the feel of each rock, the quality of the sunlight, the texture of the subsoil and the condition of my lower back to dictate the final design of a rock wall. Sometimes I can't wait to see how my creations turn out, to reach that tactile moment when enough work has been done that the rest can be envisioned. The garden allows me to be both working artist and interested spectator. That simultaneity is part of the rich and transformative experience of personal landscape architecture.

Our town's many rock retaining walls were built several decades ago by members of the Italian community. Made from quarried granite, they set a very high standard of stability, elegance, and almost Incan precision. Carmelo, one of the neighbourhood patriarchs, used to come over and observe my amateur wallbuilding. He never offered any criticism; it was plain to both of us that he didn't need to. As I was excavating for a new terrace, I unearthed a massive boulder that was exactly in the wrong place, and after considerable struggle, I realized I couldn't move it. So I brought out my sledgehammer and went to work. The repeated blows produced a nice melodic ring, and a few tiny granite flakes, but nothing else. No hairline cracks, no fissures, no sign that the great rock might be weakening. My sledgehammer just bounced off, and it seemed to travel faster on the rebound than on the downswing. Carmelo came by, and observed gravely as I hammered away and poured sweat. "Sledgehammer too small, you rest five minutes," he said, and left. He returned with a monster sledge with a bright yellow fibreglass handle. I'd never seen such a thing. "*Quattordici libra*, fourteen pounds," he said. "Yours maybe six." He stepped back while I hefted the leviathan hammer. I took an experimental swing, just to get the hammer's heft, and then gave it the full windup, and let fly. With a resounding crunch, the massive hammer engaged the boulder, getting its full attention. This sledge stayed exactly where it landed, instead of bouncing off crazily, like mine did. Three more swings, and I saw a definite seam developing. Ten minutes later the boulder was in manageable pieces, and I gratefully handed the sledge back to Carmelo. Without a trace of condescension, he offered parting advice.

"Easy to remember. Big rock, big tool."

My rock walls show a progression in skill level from the awkward first attempts to the most recent. But no matter how uniformly they are made, all rock walls offer pleasing variation in colour, texture and shape. I used to dream of a flat yard to work with. Now I think if I had one, I would dig it up just so I could terrace and build rock walls.

Artificial edges, like my rock walls, are places of excess. Edges in nature, on the other hand, are about resource limits. Natural edges are those ragged, arbitrary affairs where moisture, or seeds, or soil nutrients drop below some critical threshold. Sometimes they are associated with dramatic slope breaks or barriers, but more often they are not. Ecologists spend a lot of time attempting to define and predict communities and their boundaries, without much success. Gardeners on the other hand, know their edges intimately and place them according to a template that refers to nature in some way. But templates imply order, and nature loves chaos as much as order: native plant communities can be both sophisticated and random at the same time. A Minnesota ecologist by the name of David Tilman was intrigued with the plant associations he found in some relic tallgrass prairie communities. He wondered why certain native wildflowers were found in one area, but not in other areas with very similar soils and topography. He set about collecting seeds of these wildflowers, scattered them in areas where they were absent and sure enough, a few years later they had become part of the flora. What this suggested to Tilman is that the wildflowers were distributed not by an orderly biological process, but by a kind of random postglacial crapshoot. They might find their own way to the new areas eventually, but so far they simply hadn't had the time. Or the inclination. Such is the delicious ambiguity of ecology; we're never really sure whether natural communities are purposeful or accidental.

As I bring new plants into my yard I often think of David Tilman, that accomplished teller of ecological stories. If it is true that nature can occasionally suffer from Arrested Development, then as gardener and landscaper, I can be a kind of one-on-one tutor, helping to move things along. The trick is to remain humble enough to remember that in nature, the slapdash and the haphazard coexist with elegantly purposeful complexity.

One of the big reasons for maintaining so many edges in my yard is for good treasure hunts. Birthdays, until my children grew up, were always an occasion for these arranged adventures. Spud the dog and I would prepare the hunt by putting the first clue — a small, folded piece of paper — at the traditional place, under a brass water faucet by the front door. That clue provided cryptic directions to the next clue, which we had tucked away in some other part of the yard, and so on and so on until the last clue led the hyperactive birthday mob to the hidden loot bags. One year I did succumb to the temptation to turn the treasure hunt into a botany lesson ("take ten steps from the peonies and look under the euonymus"), but the kids gave it overwhelmingly negative reviews.

Pathways, raised beds, rock walls and massed plantings — lots of edge, in other words — make for much more satisfactory treasure and Easter egg hunt terrain than does a flat and featureless lawn. These elements also help to remind the parents, as they watch the kaleidoscopic gaggle of birthday children foraying back and forth, that with the right eyes, even a small yard can become a whole universe. This sense of the vast within the small comes easily to the young and to the very old; the rest of us have to work at it.

Meadow is another edge template, a more boreal one. Like savanna, it has profoundly influenced our landscaping. Meadows — pockets within a forest that are held in a treeless state — are usually creations of moisture. Either too much, too little or the wrong kind. Trees will always crowd a meadow, towering over and leaning in, just as grass crowds the garden edge. Shrubs are often able to go further out toward the centre of the meadow than trees can. So the ensemble of meadow vegetation, as seen through the eyes of the ecologist as well as the landscaper, is richly layered. In the centre of the meadow are low forbs and grasses, then shrubs at middle distance and behind it all, a rich and verdant scrim of trees. Meadows layer in a vertical sense, whereas the savanna's layers lie parallel to the horizon. Those fortunate to have enough room, and even some of us that don't, often work to the meadow example in our domestic landscaping.

Adding water to the foreground of the meadow, in the form of pond, lake or river, completes a compelling riparian visual tableau that was used to great effect by the French landscape painter Claude Monet. They say Monet was a painter of light, but he was also a master of edges, both landscaped and natural. Willows bending over a quiet pond — the interface between land and water — was a favourite theme that the Impressionist painter came back to over and over again.

There is a profoundly restful quality to Monet's paintings of ponds, waterlilies, densely vegetated shorelines and overhanging willows. When I think of the ultimate source of these landscape elements, the riparian zones of nature, I can understand this restfulness. Slow-moving or still water, floating aquatic vegetation, and mature, overhanging trees are all hallmarks of a rich, stable and late seral ecosystem, one far removed from turmoil, catastrophic disturbance and dread. It is no wonder that Monet reproductions are so often found in waiting rooms.

The great irony of Monet's famous waterlily paintings is that he designed and built the pond they grew in, and planted the waterlilies. He invested great effort to maintain plants, water and trees in just the right arrangement, just so he could paint the scene over and over again, in different shades of summer light. In 1910, the nearby River Epte flooded and destroyed much of the constructed water garden, but the painter patiently rebuilt it. Monet's waterlily paintings are masterworks of colour, composition and technique, but they also portray a unique masterwork of built ecology.

Plants and landscapes are a wonderful source of art inspiration. I once had a virulent case of writer's block, which left me unable to write a thing, until I discovered the greenhouse cure. I happened to be visiting an arboretum, and was so enchanted with the tropical greenhouse that I sat down on a secluded bench to enjoy the atmosphere. Dense, layered foliage surrounded me, and the humid air somehow moistened my desiccated literary membranes. Almost without thinking, I brought out my notebook and reeled off page after page. It was awesome. A week later, I tried another greenhouse, to make sure the first experience wasn't just a pleasant fluke, and the words flowed equally well. I made sure my recovery was total, since tropical greenhouses are not readily available writing venues. I now dream of building a small greenhouse for myself, in case the dreaded block attacks again. Oh, and for the plants, too.

It is difficult to say where the structural patterns of nature leave off, and where human landscape art and aesthetics begin. How do we distinguish, ecologically and aesthetically, between Monet's lily pond, and a natural pond that happens to grow waterlilies? Is there a harmonic convergence between the beautiful and the natural? Art is seen as a uniquely human process; it is assumed to lie dormant inside us, and artists are those who find a pathway to the inner sanctum, to awaken their muse. Might the actual origins of art lie outside the human, in the rich patterns of nature, but we appropriated them so long ago we have forgotten the source? We do have within us a far stronger intuitive sense of landscape ecology, of the rightness and wrongness of natural arrangements, than we give ourselves credit for. It is truly a tangled garden, of many edges.

Weeds "R" Us

FOR SOME YEARS I shared an office with a very dedicated weed control specialist, who ruined my family vacations. She explained to me how roads and highways are ideal corridors for weed invasion, and that in fact, the whole overarching theory of weed ecology could be demonstrated in a hundred meters of road allowance. She would point out, in excruciating detail, how roadside shoulders and ditches have soft, continuously disturbed soil, little competing vegetation, and plenty of extra moisture. How roadsides are elevated above the surrounding terrain, so they capture more of the sun's heat. How travellers from near and afar continuously introduce new species into the rich roadside environment. She actually went as far as comparing a roadside to a raised-bed garden.

My office mate specialized in biological control of weeds, and she was completely devoted to the subject. Often I would arrive at work in the morning, to find my desk covered with plastic buckets filled with the latest insect introduction, destined for release on knapweed or Dalmatian toadflax. If I complained, she would respond by saying, "No Gayton, those are not *maggots*, they are root-feeding *larvae*, and the job they are going to do is far more important than whatever it is you do. So shut up and take a pill."

In spite of the forced indoctrination, I have grown to love weeds. Geraniums and tomatoes don't teach me much, but weeds can teach me volumes about ecology and plant function. One of the easiest doorways into the rich kingdom of plant ecology is through the medium of these pesky plants. In their single-minded pursuit of survival, weeds use every eco-physiological trick in the book, and new editions are coming out all the time. Weeds are more than a blight and a curse: they are often signs that we are doing something wrong with the land. Weeds are a common thread between gardens, agriculture and nature (I even have a weedy algae in my aquarium). Weeds also teach me about myself, about my culture and my species, since there would be no weeds if there were no humans. Weeds, quite literally, r-us.

Dandelion was used in a classic plant ecology study: messrs Gadgil and Solbrig looked at the percentage of biomass this plant devoted to reproduction in disturbed sites, and compared that reproductive commitment to dandelions growing in undisturbed sites. The disturbance-site dandelions committed huge resources to reproduction (so-called r-selectors) while the undisturbed-site dandelions (k-selectors) devoted most of their efforts to producing leaves and roots. The dandelion is indeed a superstar, a role model that other weeds can look up to.

Weeds are about invasions, and invasions are about difference. If plant communities were the same in areas of the world that shared a similar climate, then there would be no weed invasions. For such a massive and universal problem, I am always surprised by how little official attention weed invasions get. They tend to be mentioned by the news media towards the end of the hour, when some obscure scientist from a distant university gets eighteen seconds of airtime to describe the dire consequences if introduced species X, which is on the march, reaches habitat Y.

Biological invasions are actually happening right underneath our noses, all the time. Given the right frame of mind, the study of invasion can be quite fascinating, and can actually shed light on its opposite, rarity. Whatever trait that is broadly expressed and adaptable in the weed, such as its response to temperature variation, is likely to be narrow and rigidly fixed in the rare plant. Environments that weeds like are generally anathema to rare plants. The prissy elegance of rare plant study is offset by the plebeian, dirt-commonness of weed science.

Every growing region, and every garden, has its perfect weed. An introduced campanula is mine. Far back in my yard's protean stage, when it was little more than lilac hedge, grass, and the mountain ash, I discovered a sweet and nameless little herb growing in deep shade under the lilacs. It had lovely heart-shaped leaves on stalks that arose directly from the ground. Since I live in a forested region, I was quite sure this was some shy violet or ginger that had found my yard to its liking. I was honoured when it timidly began venturing beyond the lilac hedge to other shady corners of the yard. Then it started showing up in the flowerbeds and walkways, and I got a little concerned, particularly when I discovered how difficult it was to get its tough, swollen crown out of the ground.

Meanwhile, an obvious new weed had invaded my yard, sporting triangular leaves on a long central stalk, which was topped off with purple, bell-shaped flowers. It was pretty, but its behaviour instantly rang several of the weed alarm bells my office-mate had taught me. The plant was adventive, it spread rapidly, the flower stalks developed almost overnight, and the fulsome blooms held the promise of thousands of seeds. I ripped these bellflower plants out as I spotted them, wondering as I did so why I saw only mature specimens, and never seedlings. The ecological wheels in my mind slowly began to turn. Bearings squealed, belts slipped, cylinders misfired, but finally the gears of understanding meshed: the supposed shy forest violet I was encouraging was actually the wildly different rosette phase of the weedy bellflower. *Campanula rapunculoides*, the books called it: creeping bellflower, or more melodiously, rampion. By the time this noxious Eurasian biennial bolts, the sweet little rosette leaves have withered away, and the plant takes on a totally different look.

Following my personal principle that new information always comes with unexpected tangents worthy of exploration, I looked further into the nature of rampion. Like the mountain ash, I found it overladen with medieval and mythical lore. Rapunzel was named after it. Children in medieval Italy were said to quarrel after coming in contact with it. Decoctions of its leaves were good for "maladies of the throte." Rampion lore was so fascinating that it threatened to divert me from the actual rampion invasion.

What profound transformations plants can undergo! This rampion, this trickster, went from a stemless, shade-bound, round-leaved rosette to robust, triangular-leaved and sunloving bolt. One of the rampion's favoured locations is underneath my hydrangeas. The leaves grow large and mimic the hydrangea to the point that I have to look closely to tell them apart. It is difficult to reject the notion of ecological deviousness here; my inner science geek says no, but in my gut I know the fiendish rampion deliberately set out to trick me.

For every introduced weed, there is often a close cousin that is native to North America. This complicates identification as well as control, since anything that will suppress or kill the weed is likely to do the same thing to the native species. In one of my long-term grassland plots, I was bedevilled by the presence of two annual vetches, one native and one introduced. Taxonomically, the two were separated by mind-numbingly fine details. I finally was able to separate them by simply stepping back and picking out the more vigorous plants, which were invariably the introduced species.

Weeds that are similar to cultivated plants often get an ecological free ride, which is proof that mimicry is one of the higher forms of deviousness. Wild oats are the classic of the mimic genre, reproducing virtually every aspect of the cultivated wheat, barley and oat crops it invades in such devastating fashion. Almost everything we do to favour the crop favours the weed as well. Another form of weed deviousness is beauty. Many of our noxious weeds are horticultural introductions gone rogue, as is the case with my rampion. Short of beauty, there is also nostalgia: it is hard to accept the notion of some immigrant pining away for the likes of Old World chicory, or knapweed, or morning glory, but so be it.

The rampion, in its own way, is fighting for its very existence. It was unique to my yard and, unlike the hops, is not found elsewhere in the neighbourhood. If I am successful in eliminating rampion (please God, make it happen), the species loses an important beachhead. So it fights hard for a continuing role in my garden.

The great irony of the rampion's determined attack is that its victory would be fleeting. If I gave up and surrendered my garden territories to the rampion, it would have two spectacular seasons, or five, or maybe even ten. Its very abundance might attract a predator, or a disease. Its very invasion inevitably prepares the ground for something else. Who knows what that might be; maybe western red cedar. Succession is an elegantly complex series of pathways, plateaux, loopbacks, blind alleys and surprises.

My natural approach to gardening is somewhat laid back, but when it comes to weeds, I am moving toward a scorched-earth, genocidal policy. I have suffered too many dastardly deeds at the hands of these plants. Whenever I catch myself idly pulling a weed here and there, I stop immediately and mark out a space, however small, from which I methodically rip out every single weed, suspicious plant, Kentucky bluegrass and unauthorized seedling. This sets up a kind of creative tension, since I value my garden as a space for unfocussed and uncritical enjoyment, but successful weed control requires ice-cold rationality. The ideal gardening personality is probably a mix of hippie, planner, and military strategist.

One of the best ways to control weeds is to beat them at their own game; plant something even more aggressive than the weed is, but make sure that planted competitor doesn't turn on you. When I seeded my white Dutch clover pasture under the grape arbour, plenty of rampion rosettes lurked about. They are now almost entirely gone from the little sward, smothered by the aggressively well-mannered clover.

The climate of my region is uniquely adapted to conifers, and the big balsam fir in my backyard is abundant proof of that. It receives runoff from the roof and grows a couple of meters a year. In an effort to slow its growth, I trimmed its bottom branches off, leaving a bare trunk. That of course did nothing, since new growth in conifers is supplied almost entirely from the upper branches. So I waited until my wife was away for a day, rented a pruning saw on a long extension pole, and made some partial sawcuts in the main stem, way up near the top of the tree. My theory was that the sawcuts would cause the balsam's growing tip would wither and die slowly, leaving the rest of the tree intact, but unable to grow further. When the top death became evident to Judy, I could explain it by citing an attack of the quilted balsam lopper, a dreaded forest pest. However, a mere two days later, things went awry. A brief but violent windstorm came through and snapped the balsam's top right off. I had to quickly change my story to how all that excess moisture had created weak spots in the wood. I was only partly believed.

Of course the balsam continued to grow, but now with five crowns instead of one.

My next stratagem to control the tree was to dig up a remnant of the euthanized English ivy (which of course never completely died) and plant it at the base of the tree. The ivy is now eagerly growing up the trunk, and the balsam fir is about to experience the grim reality of competition. I feel like a ju-jitsu master, having turned my enemies against each other.

Weeds make gardens look messy, and they compete with our planted ornamentals and vegetables. But mostly they are an affront because they tell us — in fact they advertise to the whole neighbourhood — that we are not in full control of what goes on in our yards and gardens. In fact, they advertise that we are probably inside drinking beer and watching football games, rather than weeding.

There is something implacable, even frightening about the ability of weeds to survive and reproduce. A while back I took advantage of a pleasant summer evening to walk downtown to see Steven Spielberg's *War of the Worlds*. As I walked slowly home from the movie, my head was filled with the echoes of Morgan Freeman's spectacular rumbling voice-overs, describing the movie's alien invaders: relentless, implacable, ruthless, beyond understanding. I looked up from my post-movie ruminations to see a two meter high clump of *Impatiens glandulifera*, or policeman's helmet, in someone's garden. The *War of the Worlds* had pumped me full of alien paranoia, and I contemplated the glistening, absurdly healthy impatiens with dread. It looked positively relentless, implacable, ruthless and beyond understanding. Could this be the next local invader, in our lengthy tradition of horticultural escapes?

We actually know a fair bit about the history of this annual impatiens. Discovered in 1839 by plant explorers in the western Himalayan region of India, seeds were brought back to Kew Gardens for multiplication. Gardeners were impressed by its spectacular growth rate, and showy (some would say gaudy) flowers. A mere twenty-five years later, impatiens was being reported as an escape along English riverbanks and ditches. The plant now holds a very high ranking on Britain's Noxious Weed List, but so far in my home region it has only received the lowly status of Common Nuisance.

Some recent North American weed research suggests that the time between arrival and invasion is on the order of six decades. Just like the menacing aliens in Spielberg's movie, the weeds are already here, lurking among us, just waiting to go rogue. And like the movie's death-dealing tripods, they seem to have boundless energy, but it turns out that it is *our* energy they are looking for. They want, as the old movie phrase goes, to suck our blood. In the case of invading weeds, they will suck the blood of our ecological integrity.

In our evolving relationship with nature, there was a period beginning in the late 1940s where total control and dominance was the ideal. Splendid new technologies were there to give us that convenient control and free us for higher pursuits, such as watching football games. With the help of the herbicide industry, we deluded ourselves into believing in the magic bullet — the ideal chemical that is lethal to one single class of organisms and has absolutely no effect on any others. What a supreme piece of human arrogance that was, to think that at the cellular level we have nothing in common with dandelions. I do look forward to the day when we no longer use herbicides on our yards and gardens. My colleagues tell me that agricultural and industrial use of herbicides is now tightly regulated, with training and environmental standards in place, and that the lawn and garden use is the only remaining unregulated sector of the herbicide market.

In suburban neighbourhoods, it is a common sight to see the householder patrolling the front yard, squirt bottle of herbicide in hand, spraying individual dandelions. That is a poor form of entertainment (which is what it is, since you can never completely eliminate dandelions). These folks need to know that employing a digging fork and a dachshund is far more fun.

The "better living through chemistry" era is having a long sunset, but it will happen eventually. My gardening hat goes off to the Province of Quebec, which at this writing is moving towards the first North American restrictions on the non-farm use of herbicides. They are in for a tough fight.

My arsenal for the weed war is pretty basic. I have my hands, the dandelion fork, a scythe and a Dutch hoe. Henry David Thoreau mused about this implement while in his garden, wondering what gave him the right to "make invidious distinctions with his hoe," choosing which plants should live, and which should die. I have none of Mr. Thoreau's qualms.

The modern definition of a weed is "a plant growing in the wrong place," and no plant fits that description better than our friend Kentucky bluegrass, which of course did not originate in Kentucky, but in central Europe. The primary component of untold millions of North American lawns, parks and golf courses, Kentucky bluegrass also invades native grasslands, gardens and flagstone-lined walkways. Every second year, I have to sharpen my Dutch hoe and laboriously shave off the linear mounds of grass that spontaneously develop between my flagstones. The grass comes off in long, ropy skeins, held together by a durable mixture of roots and rhizomes. As I rip these apart and feed them into the compost bin, I am struck by the amount of fine, dark soil that is held in the root and rhizome matrix. It can't be soil brought up from underneath the flagstones, otherwise the whole walkway would have collapsed into a sinkhole years ago.

This is soil that the bluegrass has somehow *created* from it's own biological turnover.

Some time ago, science fiction writers coined the term "terraforming", or building earth environments on other planets. In the predictable course of fantasy creating reality, terraforming is now being seriously discussed by space scientists, but the processes they propose involve elaborate chemical factories, biodomes or nuclear fission. The terraformers need to step back and consider the merits of Kentucky bluegrass.

Some introduced weeds have been with us so long that they almost qualify for landed immigrant status, if not full ecological citizenship. Common mullein (*Verbascum thapsus*) is such a candidate. Unmistakable with its broad, woolly leaves and towering, yellow-flowered seedstalk, it straddles the boundary between garden ornamental and roadside weed. We know mullein came from Europe originally, since the Italian painter Caravaggio inserted this distinctive plant into his 1604 painting, *Saint John the Baptist*. And we also know that mullein was well established in eastern North America by 1855, since Walt Whitman sees it as one of the limitless creations of God in his epic poem, "Leaves of Grass". It would be hard to find a North American jurisdiction between the Yukon and central Mexico that doesn't grow mullein. The means by which the plant might have gotten to North America are legion, and probably not worth speculating on.

I usually leave one or two of the mullein rosettes I find in my garden. These biennial plants are interesting if not attractive, and the durable seed stalk, which retains its tiny, oily seeds, is an instant no-hassle winter bird feeder. And incidentally, the broadly oval (oblanceolate is the nitpicky term) leaves have soft, felt-like hair, and make an excellent hiker's substitute for forgotten toilet paper.

Baby's breath (*Gypsophila paniculata*) is a favourite of the florist trade, but it can also a vicious weed. There is a story about how the plant got its first toehold in the Canadian prairies, in about 1980. West of Moose Jaw, Saskatchewan, the Trans-Canada Highway passes through a belt of sandy soil, which baby's breath dearly loves. Some passing traveller tired of a florist's wedding or funeral bouquet and tossed it out the window, releasing a few baby's breath seeds in the process. A year later, when the one or two roadside plants that started from that original bouquet were in their full glory, someone else stopped to pick a few stems. About a kilometre further down the highway that traveller discovered just how unpleasant the odour of fresh baby's breath can be, and chucked it out the window. Other travellers repeated the process and soon Saskatchewan had an absolutely linear invasion of baby's breath, about twenty kilometres long. As far as I know, it is still there.

This story actually relates to how my former colleague ruined my family vacations. Her dedication to weeds was infectious, and she pimped me into watching the edge of the highway for range extensions and new invaders. Now I can't drive anywhere in the summer without engaging in a continuous and compulsive scan of the roadside. (I keep a sharp eye out for suitable stones for my rock walls as well.) It doesn't matter that I have developed the unique talent to be able to distinguish diffuse knapweed from spotted knapweed at a hundred kilometres an hour, or that I know precisely the current boundaries of an orange hawkweed invasion. This is not the stuff of pleasant family conversations.

THE MOVEMENT OF PLANTS

A NATIVE SHRUB grows in my garden. Sprawling, evergreen and stemmy, it is an oddity, not fitting any of the standard categories of ornamental. I remember the day I planted it and the hopes that went with it, my first native planting. Spud and I dug a very large hole for the shrub, to give this unknown quantity as much freedom as possible to explore its new home and settle in.

Although he can be destructive on occasion, it is a pleasure to watch Spud dig; he was born to it. His digging cycle starts with a kind of stationary pounce, as he thrusts his short front legs into the dirt. Then the muscles across his broad back engage, and tractor-like, he drags a load of dirt backward out of the hole with his paws, finishing with a fling that sends the dirt flying out between his hind legs. Before that load has hit the ground, he is well into the next pounce. His digging is totally pointless, since there are no badgers or ground squirrels in the garden, but it is intensely purposeful. If I take him to the beach, he immediately starts a trenching project in the sand, which continues until we go home. When we dig in the garden, I like to think of him as my assistant. I'm sure he feels the same way about me.

. The story of this native shrub started with a pleasant and mysterious odour. I am a habitué of mature ponderosa pine forests, which are North America's secular cathedrals. Light filters down through their high and open crowns as through stained glass. Sacred music is provided by wind through the canopy, and cicadas. The fragrant air of old-growth ponderosa pine forests carries a blend of vanilla, a dash of grass hay, and a leaven of something else, a kind of delicate sandalwood odour. I knew the source of the vanilla, having often buried my nose in the ponderosa's rough and fragrant bark. And the origin of the hay smell, for a grassland ecologist, was a dead giveaway. But the source of the sandalwood odour eluded me.

After a long process of observation, elimination and sniffing, I finally connected this subtle, resinous fragrance to a particular evergreen-leaved shrub found in ponderosa pine forests, one I had obviously seen before, but never took notice of.

Identifying a new native plant can be a quick and painless process, when someone points it out for you on the spot, or you make a lucky hit in the plant book. But more often the connection builds slowly. First there is a kind of individualization, where a set of identifying characteristics — like shiny evergreen leaves, small white flowers and a sandalwood smell — begin to set a plant apart from the chaotic green sea of botany that surrounds us. These characteristics may flit along the edges of our awareness for a time. Next will come the shock of multiple recognitions, when we realize we have already experienced those same shiny leaves and white flowers and sandalwood smell in other locations. After that comes the difficulty of actually identifying the unknown plant, and committing the identification to memory. The way this process works in my own head reminds me of an elaborate nonsense machine, cobbled together from bicycle parts and inexpensive kitchen appliances. There is a lot of extraneous mental clanking and banging, and I believe a cuckoo clock is involved.

In one of those season-long plant identification processes, I finally came to know the sandalwood-smelling shrub as snowbrush (*Ceanothus velutinus*), also known as buckbrush, tobaccobrush, or eponymously, ceanothus. Once the identification process was complete and I knew what this sprawling, evergreen-leaved shrub was, I saw it often, nearly always in the company of ponderosa pine. It was the provider of holy aromas to the ponderosa cathedrals. Reading more (a weakness), I discovered that snowbrush is one of those unique plants, like the legumes, that cultivates a relationship with friendly bacteria that take nitrogen directly from the air. This plant in effect, "sponsors its own fertility," to quote Wendell Berry. And further, it seems to join its roots with those of the ponderosa, exchanging unknown substances for the mutual benefit of both.

A plant of so many resonating layers cried out for possession: I wanted a snowbrush for my very own. Ecologists have much in common with power shoppers, but their consumer impulses play out in odd ways, like desperately wanting a *Ceanothus velutinus* for their yard. Fortunately, my newly identified native plant of the moment was not rare. In addition to growing in ponderosa forests, it tended to colonize certain disturbed, gravelly banks. After some looking, I found a suitable snowbrush on a roadcut and was able to dig it out without adding significantly to the general level of human devastation of native ecosystems. Carefully preserving a large root ball as I excavated, I was certain that some of the friendly bacteria would accompany the snowbrush to its new suburban home.

My north-facing yard is more cedar forest than ponderosa pine habitat, so I chose an exposed, sunny, west-facing location along the driveway, and lovingly planted the snowbrush along with its precious bacteria. Spud helped me mix the native soil into my garden soil. For the next three years the plant did absolutely nothing, not dying but steadfastly refusing to grow. In year four it unexpectedly took hold, putting out lustrous new leaves and a modest spray of tiny, fragrant flowers. Now every summer my mundane driveway smells unexpectedly of ponderosa pine forest. The rule of thumb for planted natives is sleep in the first year, creep in the second year, leap in the third year. My ceanothus took two sleep years.

Moving plants from one place to another is a primordial human urge, not to be denied. In fact, gardening, landscaping and even agriculture are mere incidental side effects of our compulsion to move plants. The results of this urge are variously spectacular and insidious, magnificent and corrosive, noble and criminal. The drive to collect, move and scatter seed goes right to the heart of our relationship with nature. We have believed all along, and apparently still do, that the local ecosystem we live in is somehow poorly constructed, lacking in key species and not nearly as attractive or productive as the local ecosystem we recently moved from, have read about, or dreamed about.

My own home province, British Columbia, has been a major donor as well as recipient of intercontinental plant traffic. David Douglas, the eminent Scottish botanist, brought dozens of British Columbia species back to Europe in the 1830's. Two of his tree introductions, Sitka spruce and his namesake, the Douglas-fir, formed the basis for Scottish industrial forestry, much to the detriment of the native Scottish tree species.

Another Douglas, no relation to David, was active in the plant trade. The Scot Sir James Douglas, first Governor of British Columbia, apparently found the rare and spectacular Garry oak meadow ecosystems of southern Vancouver Island to be sadly lacking. In 1851, upon taking up his duties in the lovely parklike environs of Victoria, full of blue camas and elegant fescue, he sent this note to Colonial authorities in London:

"I forward a small requisition for various kinds of grass seeds which I beg be forwarded by the first ship bound for the Island."

Modern ecological restorationists in both Vancouver Island and in Scotland are almost completely blocked in their attempts to restore even small parcels of native ecosystems, because of the overwhelming presence of introduced species. Ironically, the introduced European orchardgrass (*Dactlyis glomerata*), undoubtedly part of James Douglas' seed requisition, is an invasive and persistent colonizer of Garry oak meadows in and around Victoria.

Johnny Appleseed, the American folk hero, personifies the messianic urge to transplant. Mr. Appleseed might have thought he was bringing New England flora to the American Midwest, but he was actually just another bit player in a centuries-long saga of incremental apple dispersion, starting from the tree's original home in Kazakhstan.

The area where I live, near the confluence of the Kootenay and Columbia rivers, was once famous for its cherry orchards, but a wealthy impresario helped put a stop to that. Canadian engineer Selwyn Blaylock (1879-1945) founded Cominco, a highly successful mining and smelting business, and with the profits he built a fine Tudor-style mansion and grounds along the shores of the Kootenay River. A devoted gardener, Blaylock began planting the grounds with ornamental trees of every description. He had his heart set on including a particular ornamental cherry from Asia, but plant quarantine authorities refused to let him import it, citing the potential for disease transmission to cultivated cherries. Not one to be deterred by petty bureaucrats in the obscure Department of Agriculture, Blaylock simply smuggled the ornamental cherry tree in, thus unleashing "little cherry disease", a virus that made short work of the orchards in the area.

I think of this story whenever I am about to dig a plant up from the wild and bring it home to my garden. Will this delicate thing turn into a monster? The Selwyn Blaylock story carries two important messages for gardeners: do your research first, and don't bring arrogance into the garden.

As I pursue the slow process of recognizing and committing plants to memory, I am surprised by the number of local native species that also show up in the black plastic pots of the greenhouse trade. That should be a good sign, but somehow the purchase of an Oregon grape in a nursery is not looping back to a greater awareness of the incredibly adaptable Oregon grape in the wild.

Native plant advocates like myself are conflicted: we strive for a greater appreciation of our native plants, but get concerned as soon as people get motivated enough to go dig them up or collect seeds. Loss of genetic diversity, damage to rare or isolated populations and weed invasion from soil disturbance are all possible outcomes of wild harvest. But perhaps the biggest loss is to the plant itself, since transplants usually die and seeds frequently rot before they germinate.

Wild harvest of native plants needs to be put into an ethical context, and indeed, several native plant organizations have developed codes of practice. I have three personal additions to these codes.

First, do your research. Native plants often have very specific requirements for soil type, nutrition, and microclimate. Once I transplanted a lovely grassland penstemon into my garden and watched it decline slowly, with less new growth each spring. In surfing the research literature one day, I discovered the likely reason: this particular penstemon is parasitic on sagebrush. By jacking its roots into those of a neighboring sage, it gets a free nutritional ride. With this particular penstemon I was fortunate, since someone had actually researched it and the information was readily available. Our knowledge of the requirements and life cycle of a native plant is far more likely to be a blank slate.

Second, do your harvest in already disturbed areas, like cutblocks, roadcuts, construction sites and road allowances. Or harvest in areas about to be disturbed. Going in just ahead of the bulldozer can be a satisfying — and exciting — activity.

Third, take a minority of the plant material (seeds or transplants) from a site, and don't go back to the same site year after year for more material.

And fourth, if you are transplanting, dig three times deeper than you think you need to, and get the entire taproot. I made the mistake once of choosing a sandy cutbank to get a ponderosa pine seedling, because the digging would be so easy. But attached to this meter-high seedling was a taproot the thickness of a garden hose that went straight down to somewhere near the Cretaceous.

And fifth, think about season. Typically the flowering period is when we see plants and want them, but it is the worst time for transplanting, since warm weather has already arrived, and the plant has already shifted from vegetative to reproductive growth. Better to mark the plant in the summer, and come back as early as possible the next spring, to transplant it. That leaves the winter for research, and anticipation.

Another native species in my garden is the lovely blue-flowered camas, part of the lily family. Essentially a coastal plant in western North America, it has an odd, disjunct distribution in the Interior, found in certain wet meadows and riparian areas. The camas may have been the first crop plant of the Pacific Northwest; its bulbs were a staple food for native people, and they were easily dug and transplanted. I collected my camas from a thriving population at the junction of the Kootenay and Columbia rivers, a fishing location favoured by First Nation people for millennia. It is not much of a logical leap to assume that most, if not all, the populations of camas in the BC Interior were introduced as supplemental food sources. It gives me pleasure to carry that tradition onward, in some small way.

This year spring is advancing quickly, so Spud and I are out working in the yard early. The dandelions are quite deficient at this time of year, and there are very few with the thick taproots he so favours. When I do find a few that overwintered under the protection of the peonies or behind a shrub, his joy is unmistakable. But he shreds them quickly, and to avoid his peremptory barks for more, I clean out lawn borders, an activity which generates fetchable clumps of invading bluegrass. After those are all dug out, caught and shredded, I am forced to improvise, bridging our way to the dandelion season by flinging twigs or tennis balls. I don't know whether this odd dog behaviour is play or obsession, and I'm not sure Spud knows, either.

Always a sucker for species lore, I did some reading on my dog's breed. "Dachshunds have an intense desire to prevail," stated one dog expert, who wrote as though he hoped to avoid lawsuits. Another book went into detail about the dog's badger hunting origins. Dachshunds are persistent above and below ground, it said. And their powerful bark was a feature that allowed the master to know what was going on, even when the dog was deep in the ground.

On a recent grassland walk, I was able to show Spud an active badger den. He was totally uninterested.

A colleague of mine, fellow dachshund owner and serious fisherman, corroborated the breed's misplaced retrieving syndrome. His dog's obsession is fish. Little Maxie watches every cast intently, is galvanized by the sound the reel makes after a strike, and goes completely bonkers when his master lands a fish.

Spud the dog is my garden companion, my noisy one-dog Greek chorus. I address deep eco-philosophical questions to his squat form as we dig or weed. Spud is part of a long and honourable tradition of nonhuman garden companionship. The English ur-naturalist Gilbert White had such a companion in the form of a pet Mediterranean tortoise, which patrolled his garden from 1780 until a year after White's death in 1793. In his classic *Natural History of Selborne*, White delights in describing Timothy the tortoise's movements, which garden plants he favoured, and how he reacted to the weather.

Our ancestors began selecting and moving plants for agriculture about ten millennia back in time. Less than a historical heartbeat later, they started right into gardening and landscaping. The two centres of origin of the craft of gardening appear to be ancient Egypt and China, around five thousand years ago. The first recorded ornamental plant hunting expedition was organized by Egyptian Queen Hatsheput in 3500 BP, when she sent ships to the coast of East Africa to bring back specimens of *Boswellia*, the frankincense tree, to grace her gardens at Karnak. Hatsheput would be pleased to know that she was a trendsetter. She pioneered the activity of ornamental plant hunting, which has given purpose to the lives of countless adventurers, fools, miscreants, merchants and obsessives right down to the present day. People like William Dampier, who successfully combined plant collecting with high-seas piracy. Or William Arthur, who broke his leg while collecting lilies in the high mountains of China. As Mr. Arthur's companions carried him down a very narrow and precipitous mountain path, they met a mule pack train coming the other way. The travel impasse was resolved by lying the splinted botanist crosswise on the path, and then having all fifty mules carefully step over him, while he held his precious lily bulbs tightly to his chest.

The discovery of a new ornamental plant has triggered social upheavals. Carolus Clusius, a modest botanist who saw much of 17th century Europe while dodging religious persecution, brought tulips back from the ornamental gardens of Turkey. Thinking he had found a safe haven as director of a small botanical garden in Holland, he set about planting and cultivating his tulips. When he declined to sell them, jealous entrepreneurs broke into Clusius' research garden at night and stole his bulbs, thus initiating the famous "tulipmania" frenzy, which by contrast, made the Alaska Gold Rush look like a carefully organized event.

The halcyon period of plant hunting was undoubtedly the nineteenth century, when the efforts of European scientists and adventurers brought the list of available garden plant species from a few dozen to the thousands we have available to us today. For many decades, Kew Gardens in London was the nerve centre of this worldwide collecting enterprise.

A thorough review of the history of plant hunting provides refreshing evidence that the human species does have the capacity to act out its fundamental irrationality in fairly harmless ways. Apparently there are one or two homicides attributed to orchid collectors, but this group has always been on the fringes, and are noted for their general excitability. Few armies employ botanists; in fact stories abound of plant hunters collecting right through active war zones, oblivious to the carnage going on around them.

However primordial the desire to move plants may be, it is probably the handmaiden of an even more basic urge — to create captive ecosystems. To pick and choose flora and fauna from diverse locations and bring them together successfully in novel arrangements, meanwhile flaunting every ecological rule in the book, is truly what we love to do best. The range of names we have for these creations is an indication of how central that synthetic activity is to our lives: park, garden, aquarium, terrarium, vivarium, zoo, farm, arboretum, vineyard, orchard, wild animal park, lawn, golf course — the list is surprisingly long.

The contemporary ecophilosopher Frederick Turner thinks we have a threefold responsibility to nature: to maintain existing ecosystems, to restore damaged ones, and to create new ones. Turner's third task is a startling idea, until one puts it in perspective. That is, in fact, what the new generation of gardeners, landscapers, and permaculturists do, as they mix native and introduced trees, shrubs, forbs and grasses in novel and sometimes bizarre combinations. Randomly planting a bunch of species together doesn't make an ecosystem, but when the landscaper/gardener takes into account niche, adaptation and esthetics, and persists with the enterprise, there is the chance to create a harmonious whole. And harmony is the mistress of ecology. Attempting to build an ecosystem is a pathway to the understanding of ecosystems, and to a sense of community with nature's enterprise. If we truly want to accept the daunting challenge of ecological restoration, and begin rebuilding damaged pieces of nature, perhaps the best way to learn is to build domestic caricatures of ecosystems first. Mother nature's apprenticeship program is a long one, and it is unfortunate that many of us, men in particular, leave gardening to the second half of our lives. That doesn't leave a lot of time to practise building ecosystems.

The cultural image of the garden is ancient. We carry it through history, location and fashion, through a thousand variants, but always there is the garden grace, and the garden constant.

Constant also is the image of the gardener, the patient nurturer, the one who stays on the margins of the world of commerce, in order to cultivate plants for our pleasure and palate. A society composed of only gardeners would inevitably collapse, but think of a society with no gardeners. It would certainly lack both grace and shallots.

When I was an impoverished grad student at the University of Saskatchewan, I normally walked to the campus except on those lip-splitting winter days when the wind blew straight down from the Arctic circle. Then I would splurge and take the bus. It was on one of those grim January days when I met a Canadian horticultural hero. It was late afternoon, dark already, and few people were on the Number Seven bus as it took its circuitous route through Saskatoon's suburbs. A slight, older gentleman sat across from me. He was well dressed, but the dark suit, wide lapels, fedora and buckle galoshes all seemed from the 1950s. Even his glasses spoke of that era. I struck up a conversation, asking him what he had been doing at the University. He replied that he was visiting the Medical School, inquiring about the new drugs that were used to overcome tissue rejection in organ transplants. This was the early Seventies, and heart transplants were much in the news. I asked him if he was a doctor, and he replied that no, he was a nurseryman.

I got off at his stop.

Percy Wright (1898-1989) turned out to be a neighbour of mine, and a man of many parts. Besides operating a nursery for years, he was a newspaperman and plant breeder. He was responsible for the development of several horticultural varieties, including the Thunderchild flowering crab, Yellow Altai and Hazeldean roses, and the Nubian lily, all capable of withstanding the unforgiving climate of the Canadian prairies. At the time, Percy was deeply into interspecific grafting, and his interest led him to speculate whether the new techniques for overcoming tissue rejection in organ transplants could be transferred to the plant world. As we got to know each other, I was struck by Percy's essential humility. Percy had omnivorous interests, and somehow our conversations were mostly me answering his questions, rather than the other way around, a fact that now mortifies me. It was a privilege to know this man who so greatly expanded the horizons of the northern prairie gardener. I have planted a yellow Altai rose in his honour.

Eden is the first garden in the Judeo-Christian imagination, but the vision of it is vague on one fundamental point: was the garden of Eden built, or was it natural? Was all nature like a garden before the Fall, or was Eden a special enclave, planted just for Adam and Eve? Did God select an ordinary planted garden, and turn it in to Eden by bestowing the gift of fruitfulness? Does a divinely planted garden become pristine nature, or does this sacred transformation happen in the reverse direction? A cultural ambiguity like this, which has endured for some two millennia, must be important, and somehow necessary. We want the tame and the wild to be interwoven.

The world's first gardens were all private and inward-looking. Even some representations of Eden show walls in the background. The original courtyards and walled gardens of Persia became the *hortus occlusus* of Medieval Europe. These were exclusive, subservient creations, not at all referential to nature, and stunningly beautiful. They, like all gardens, prompted peacefulness and reflection, but only for the select few. The world would wait many centuries before the grand tradition of public parks and gardens began.

Plant hunters have probably already found all of the world's showy native plants and moved them into the horticultural realm. But gardening is slowly moving beyond mere showiness to the appreciation of traits like local adaptation, low water demand and ecological significance. We may be seeing the beginnings of a new plant hunting era, where we forsake the high mountains of China in favour of our own local ecosystems.

I didn't go to nearly the same effort for my *Ceanothus* as Queen Hatsheput did for her *Boswellia*. She sent ships to the Land of Punt, on the east coast of Africa: I went thirty kilometres to a gravelly roadcut through a ponderosa forest. But we both collected for the same complex set of reasons, which are all captured in that most resonant of words, *garden*.

THE RHYTHM OF TREES

IN THE GRAND cycle of garden life, the dying part is always awkward. Plants that have been with us for years, faithful and steady, can weaken and die within a season. Or confidently leaf out in the spring and then suddenly collapse. Sometimes plants die from insects or disease or frost, but more often the cause of death is not immediately apparent. All gardeners find mortality and winter difficult to accept. I have a bleeding heart that every year grew more vigorous and was rapidly becoming the centrepiece of a garden bed, when suddenly it dropped back to a few spindly stems. I was alarmed at first, but then came to terms with its decline after researching its native habitat. Bleeding heart favours temporary openings in wet, coniferous forests. This is not a plant that grows in place for decades at a time. Instead, its life plan is to grow rapidly in the few years of full sunlight, and then bow out gracefully as waves of shrubs and trees recolonize the forest opening. A massive, congested root crown a foot across, which my bleeding heart had developed, would not be found in nature. So I must accept its eventual death, or intervene, break up the crown and create a series of new plants.

Gardens seem to reward hyperactive interventionists as well as the placid Buddhist types, but rarely middle-of-the-road compromisers like myself.

Not far from the bleeding heart sat my mountain ash tree, anchoring one corner of my yard. It provided this stalwart service to me as well as to previous owners of this house for several decades. I saw it from our living room window; it conveniently screened a power pole from view, and its trunk supported my hammock. Like its close relative the apple, the leaky and nutritious bark of the mountain ash harboured a vibrant collection of lichens and mosses. This tree's peak moment came in late spring every year, when a noisy, cackling horde of Bohemian waxwings appeared from out of nowhere to swarm the tree and feast on its clusters of small orange berries.

Views of lush vegetation can trigger a sense of ease and personal contentment in our minds. I feel that trigger very powerfully when I walk into a greenhouse full of tropical plants, and I know that it operates in outdoor settings as well. In a snowbound winter, the sight of my berry-choked mountain ash always triggered that sense of vegetative content. It was my beacon of lushness, of generosity, in the depths of a mean season. I think I agree with the Indian writer/philosopher Rabindranath Tagore when he said that trees were the earth's endless effort to speak to listening heaven.

But the tree was dying. Each year another branch would give up and withdraw into darkness. So I began to water it religiously. I fertilized along the dripline, I composted and I mulched, but the decline continued, inexorably. The bleeding heart's demise was explainable; this wasn't. Perhaps the cause was a subclinical drought cycle, or changes to subterranean waterflows, or surreptitious competition from my nearby shrub plantings, or invisible salt loads from the City's snow plowing. Such a dramatic decline for no obvious reason was disturbing. I decided to take action.

Twenty-five feet in the air, armed with my Swede saw and galloping acrophobia, I was fully prepared to cut away the dead branches of the mountain ash. If that didn't actually help the tree, at least it would make it look better. An hour into the pruning project, after sawing through rotten limb after rotten limb, I finally confronted the harsh fact that the tree was too far gone, and had to come down. This mountain ash had been like a river or a mountain for me — it was not supposed to go away. I couldn't decide which was the worse betrayal: my decision to cut the tree down when it was still alive, or its decision to leave me.

The yard space available in which to drop the tree was quite small. I had power lines on two sides, a lilac hedge on a third, and mugho pines on a fourth. So I had to extend the already shaky ladder even farther up the tree in order to start cutting it down in small chunks and dropping them straight down, to the patch of grass directly below. My first cut was the hardest, as the very top of the main trunk leaned toward the power lines. This took some planning, a rope anchor, and several nervous trips up and down the ladder. I could see the neighbours rolling their eyes again. Piece by piece the tree came down though, exactly according to plan.

Being endowed with a Clydesdale frame and appetite, but saddled with a sedentary lifestyle, I welcomed the opportunity to cut the tree up into firewood with my Swede saw. Like our domestic finances, my metabolic budget seems always to be running in the red.

I fight middle-age spread by occasional running or trips to the gym, but to actually commit to these sporadic exercises requires moving several tonnes of inertia first. Cutting up the mountain ash was easy by comparison. I actually looked forward to getting home from work, donning grubby clothes and bathing myself in the rank glory of sweat, sawdust and arboreal lichens. One of the neighbours came by and offered a chainsaw, but I said no, preferring instead the slow, quiet process of the Swede saw. If I was going to administer last rites to an old friend, it was going to be totally by hand. At the very thickest part of the trunk I wavered on the offer, until I thought of the early loggers in this Kootenay country, incredible athletes who ran huge handsaws all day while living on salt pork and beans. Over the course of several days, I gradually broke almost the entire tree down into neat piles of firewood, kindling, mulch and compost. I never actually lost any weight, but surely some fat must have converted to muscle.

I knew there was a native western mountain ash (*Sorbus scopulina*) as well as the introduced European mountain ash (*Sorbus aucuparia*) and that they were quite similar. Since I had never bothered to sort out the identity of my tree, I decided it was high time. Sitting down amongst the rubble of the recently fallen yard sentinel, I delved into my floras to see which one this one was. Thirteen turned out to be the key. Most of the leaves of the European mountain ash have thirteen or more leaflets (six leaflet pairs plus one terminal leaflet); the native has mostly thirteen or fewer. The flora in its own cryptic way was inviting me to do a statistical analysis. A random count of several leaves soon confirmed that my tree was the European mountain ash, also known by its ancient Celtic name of rowan.

The rowan has drawn a vast mythology unto itself, giving it more symbolic importance than perhaps any other plant species. Even the name is thought to share the same Celtic root as the word "rune," meaning mystery. Every early tribe in Europe laid down their own particular rowan stories and meanings. The point of departure for much of the mystic started with the tiny pentagram figure that can be seen on the bottom of each rowan fruit. Sailors carried a small piece of the wood (a "rowan's thumb") to avoid death by lightning at sea, since the rowan was known to thrive in craggy, lightning-prone mountaintops. Other stories have the rowan as Eve and Adam as the alder. The rowan was also known to ward off evil spirits, so it was planted in graveyards and dooryards. Because it was used to deter witches and spells in the Middle Ages, the rowan later became a suspect symbol of witchcraft during the Enlightenment. Somehow this modest tree is a compelling blank slate upon which our ancestors wrote a host of contradictory desires and fears.

Extending this lore forward, one could even imagine a system of astrology based on trees. If I wished to have my life guided by symbols, I would be far more likely to submit to the ascendance of the rowan, the oak and the ponderosa pine, than to the circumnavigations of heaven's luminaries.

So I had lost a good friend and symbolic totem, as well as a pleasant attachment point for my hammock. Like forensic evidence, the mountain ash's remains were gradually parcelled away into the woodpile and compost bin, and I even rubbed dirt into the cut stump, to make the site look less like a crime scene. But one problematic pile was left — the branches that were too thick to compost but too small for kindling wood. Every time I went by I jumped on the pile to crunch the branches down, but they remained, obdurate. In a way, this was a microcosm of the coarse woody debris paradox in dry forest ecosystems. Leaves and small-diameter material, if they are in contact with the ground, will break down fairly quickly. Large downed logs endure, and provide habitat for squirrels and salamanders. But fallen branches tend to get suspended just above the ground, out of the reach of decomposing microbes, so they endure too. But fallen branches don't provide much habitat for anything, and they go on to become a dreaded four-letter forest term: fuel.

I resolved my problematic pile by scattering it along the mulch pathway in my proposed Shady Forest Glen, between my neighbour's house and mine, where time and foot traffic gradually took care of it.

Trees celebrate years by growth rings, and the annual rings on my mountain ash's cut surfaces were plainly visible. I had saved a breast-height section of the trunk and left it by the garden bench. The tree's cross-section looked quite enchanting, so I sanded it down with increasingly finer grits of sandpaper until every elegant detail revealed itself. Darkly stained heartwood in the centre of the trunk was surrounded by blonde sapwood. Fine concentric growth rings chased each other around the tree. An old branch initial skewed the growth rings dramatically off in one direction. Here and there were sealed pockets of old insect damage. After first consulting Stokes and Smiley's classic monograph, *An Introduction to Tree Ring Dating*, I got out a magnifying glass and carefully counted the annual rings. There were seventy-eight rings, although tree seedlings are generally a few years old before they lay down the first growth ring.

This meant my tree had been planted sometime in the 1920s, which is pretty remarkable since the town was only about thirty years old at the time, and quite isolated. Silver mining provided the initial impetus for European settlement here, but that soon shifted to "fruit ranching", as the orchard industry was called in those days. Vintage photographs of the town show rows of cherry trees where neighbourhoods are now. This mountain ash must have come in on the coattails of that early fruit nursery trade.

My predecessor in this house must have gone to considerable effort to get the mountain ash, suggesting that its symbolic significance was alive and well in his or her mind, and that the easily available native mountain ash just wouldn't do.

Reading deeper into the rings, I saw that in its early years, my tree laid down a solid quarter of an inch of new wood each season. 1986, for some reason, was a banner growth year. But in the last eight years of its life, the tree's annual increments were down to paper thickness. Thinking back on the consistent abundance of its orange berries over that same span of years, I realized the sacrifice the dying tree had been making, maybe for its own rebirth, or just for the sake of the waxwings.

I left the trunk section on my garden bench for a time. It was good to sit next to it and muse on the tree's life and death, encoded in the rhythm of its rings.

❦

THE ART OF THE YARD

WHAT WE STRIVE for in garden ornamentation — from concrete frogs to wind-driven whirligigs — is both beautiful and important. Whimsy has few outlets in our society, but yard art is one, and thank God for it. The heavily ridiculed lawn gnome actually forms part of an important tradition. The socially acceptable range of lawn and garden ornamentation is surprisingly wide, and it runs from high art to conscious kitsch. Even pink flamingos are allowed, and often experience late-night ownership transfers. Sundials are a prominent feature in my yard: I have a horizontal one, with polar-pointing gnomon, and another from the armillary tradition, which is a kind of hollow brass hemisphere with an arrow through it. Both are precisely positioned so that when I stand in front of them, I can tell the time by looking at the living room clock through the front window.

Concrete birdbaths are another splendid and diverse yard genre, which I don't get to indulge in because our winter freeze-thaw cycles methodically tear them apart. I content myself instead with ornamental hummingbird feeders. And in lieu of a concrete frog, which would suffer the same fate as the birdbaths, I have the brass faucet beaver, which laughs at winter.

Our objects of yard art speak of a relaxed and elegant lifestyle, even though they mostly lie. That concrete frog, woven hammock, wind-driven whirligig or ornamental birdbath reassures us we have had sufficient time to make a whole series of esthetic decisions about choosing and placing our art object, and that we are going to be around long enough and have enough leisure time to enjoy the slow fruit of those decisions. Somehow it doesn't matter that the average adult moves every four or five years, and they can rarely spend the kind of whimsical and unfocussed time that yard art and landscaping calls for; that is not important. What *is* important is that we recognize the significance of deep garden time, the kind of time that Gilbert White spent with Timothy the tortoise. Garden produce is more than zucchinis and tomatoes; it includes esthetics, contemplation, therapy, leisure, comedy and shade. Recognizing a role for ecology in the garden also requires an acknowledgment of human ecology, as in our need for deep time.

My own attempts at garden leisure are fragmentary, and often interrupted by the dog, whose outdoor time is given over to obsession, not leisure. I circulate in the usual clockwise fashion, pulling a weed here or deadheading there, but basically idling in each separate environment I have created. Because I started from scratch, from a featureless yard, the eco-artistic responsibility for everything is mine. This has been both an opportunity and a curse. Often what I sense in my garden downtime are mere design flaws and weeds, rather than esthetic pleasures. The grape arbor, however, is a modest ecological/artistic success which I can actually enjoy. It is an airy wooden structure, about ten feet on a side and butting against a front corner of the house. During the summer the top and west face of the arbour are a mass of intertwining grape leaves and tendrils. Every spring I think about trying to make dolmades from the splendid large leaves, but then decide to leave it to the professionals at the local Greek restaurant.

One of the leisurely delights of the arbour is to place oneself along an axis between a good magnifying glass, a young grape leaf, and full sunshine. It is a revelation: laid out in the nearly transparent leaf are all the wondrous palisades and avenues of photosynthesis.

At one time I envisioned a brick patio underneath my arbour, complete with wrought iron table, checkered tablecloth and carafe of red wine. Instead I have settled for a miniature pasture of white Dutch clover, which is culturally more appropriate to the mountains of British Columbia, sustains itself quite nicely and keeps the grape quite happy. The arbour structure also forms a gateway to the narrow passage around the side of the house, where the garden shed stands. There is a step down to enter the arbour and its little postage-stamp pasture, and then another reluctant step down to leave it from the other side. Even though it is small and open to three compass aspects, the arbour feels, in landscape architecture terms, like a separate environment. I'd like to think that if the arbour was on the scale of nature, it might equate to a very simple ecosystem.

The arbour's current grape is a table variety, since I leave both winemaking and dolmades to the professionals. I started the arbour with the old reliable North American Concord, which grew like stink and promptly began to envelop my neighbour's house and mine in a furious embrace. So I planted a less aggressive variety beside it, a locally-developed variety called Coronation. Rather than ripping out the original vine, I thought I might encourage peaceful coexistence by giving the Concord a severe late spring pruning. To my dismay, the pruned stems of the Concord began weeping huge amounts of viscous, accusatory tears of sap. The vine carried on this very public display of grief for days, making it plain to the neighbours that I was not only a butcher but a sadist as well. I persisted, however. After three years of Draconian but totally ineffective pruning, I realized there was no stopping the Concord. So I finally dug out its swollen rootstock. My neighbour promptly claimed it and planted it in her yard, close to its original position.

Delivered from oppression, the Coronation is now doing well, but I watch the Concord nervously across the fence. It bides its time, building libido for another amorous assault on our two houses.

Garden beauty can often be found in the absence of ornamental intent. Garden tools are an example. They are beautiful precisely because they stand outside the realm of art, and because they have an ecology of their own. They are like sturdy country gentlemen, each with a particular skill. Resting quietly in the garden shed, they await the call to work. Over time, wooden handles develop a subtle finish from the continual rub of hands, and steel blades burnish and scallop from rhythmic contact with the earth. My own set of garden tools is fairly extensive, since I subscribe to the self-fulfilling male logic that any project worth doing deserves at least one new tool to do it with. I have two rakes, a couple of pruning saws, a trowel, small medium and large pruning shears, a disgraced sledgehammer, a mattock and a pry bar. There are three shovels — one spade, one rounded, one a narrow-bladed tree-planter type — a Dutch hoe, a pitchfork, a manual grass whip, a wooden-handled steel wheelbarrow, and a couple of buckets. The design of each one of these tools represents at least a century of continuous refinement of purpose, and none have even a speck of ornamentation. Their beauty lies in their total functionality, and the refreshing absence of microchips.

The narrow silvicultural shovel was a gift from one of my sons, since retired from the bizarre subculture of tree planting. He was careful to explain the range of tree planting shovels: there is the conventional D-handle, the Speed Shovel (short-handled for planters willing to bend over all day), and the Pottipukti, which resembles an overgrown gynaecological instrument. There is also the Rookie Shovel, an ordinary shovel totally useless for tree planting, that newbies often show up with. The long-handled one he gifted me is known as the Hippie Shovel (apparently hippies prefer not to bend over). All are characterized by heavy, narrow blades. My Hippie Shovel gets frequent use when I am transplanting shrubs and trees, since the narrow blade is very effective for cutting deep roots.

I don't look for bargains on garden tools; in fact, I tend to go the opposite direction, and buy the most expensive shovel instead of the cheapest. I share this trait with a rather traditional farmer friend who once went out to buy a replacement for a broken toaster, but came home empty-handed and furious. "I didn't want a fifteen-dollar disposable plastic toaster," he fumed, "I wanted to buy a durable toaster, a *forty-dollar* toaster, but nobody could sell me one." I saw his original toaster, the one that died. Its big, rounded lines and chrome finish anchored it solidly in the mid-1950s.

Garden tools are an arranged marriage of wood and metal, and both need maintenance. I treat the wooden handles of my tools once a year with linseed oil, to keep the wood limber and tight. And I sand them if the grain begins to raise. The handles do break occasionally, particularly on the shovels, which are built for excavation but too often get used for leverage. When I buy replacement handles, I look for strong, close-grained wood with narrow growth rings, increasingly hard to find in this age of juvenile second-growth timber. I also keep a coarse whetstone and some lubricant in the shed, to keep the shears and other bladed tools sharp. Honing blades is a shed ritual, honouring the hand tool as well as my late father, who held a lifelong reverence for tools. *Dad, you taught me well, and I want you to know that I'm still looking after your tools, and mine.*

My conscious attempts at garden beauty are often less successful than my unconscious ones. The garden shed which houses my tools has developed a brand of funky elegance all its own, an elegance that was not intended when I built it. Occupying some dead space between my neighbour's house and mine, it was cobbled together with some used mahogany panelling from a basement renovation, assorted 2 x 4s and a spare piece of linoleum. The shed is just big enough for me to stand in, alongside my country gentlemen. Inside I scabbed in a shelf to hold seed, small tools and that garden essential, extra hose washers. I also keep a notebook there, to record variety names, planting dates and impetuous literary observations that cannot wait until I get back to my desk. The shed's architecture might best be described as garden vernacular. Its location between two houses gives it some protection from the elements, which is good, because I don't think the structure would survive a windstorm or a full winter snowload on its own. I made the roof from a translucent greenhouse panel, so a bit of sun gets through to the interior. Shed ornamentation is utilitarian — a couple of decorative firebox doors scavenged from abandoned wood stoves to cover up holes in the wood panelling. A Virginia creeper is slowly embracing the shed, adding its own verdant beauty and additional structural support. The creeper, along with age and a general lack of upkeep, has allowed the shed to perform an unexpectedly graceful merger with nature.

Objects of garden art, particularly buildings, are sometimes called follies. The folly legitimacy debate has raged on for some time now; actually for a couple of centuries. Everyone agrees that a folly must have no actual function, but there are those who go on to say that any structure consciously built as a folly cannot be one, by definition. A true folly must originate from genuine but loopy intent, they say. Anything else is mere caricature. As one folly expert put it, "you cannot build one deliberately. Only other people can bestow the title of Folly on your monstrous erection."

In the early 1800s, the heyday of follies, wealthy European estate owners would create artificial lakes, and then islands in the lakes, as a site for some useless ornamental building that would provide artistic contrast with their landscaping. Faux Greek temples were popular, as were gazebos. These constructions were considered suspect by the purists, since they were not only derivative and silly in the eyes of the beholder, but those of the creator as well. So the esthetic purists coined the derogatory term *fabrique* and applied it to the structures they considered to be illegitimate follies.

The next crisis to hit the folly world was perpetrated by the landscape painters, who demanded buildings of a certain style to include in their compositions. Fortunately, aristocratic lunacy prevailed over these multiple assaults. Genuine, true follies continued to be conceived and built — in all sincerity — by eccentric nutbars.

My shed doesn't even come close to folly status — it is much too utilitarian and downscale. I have furnished it with a large spool of sisal twine, which hangs on a loop of wire along with a cheap kitchen knife to cut it with. Polypropylene twine is almost universal now, but I like the coarse, earth-toned sisal for tying up tomato plants, supporting hydrangeas or training my grapevine. Sisal twine is delightfully temporary. After a year you can break it by hand, and after three years it returns to earth, as organic matter. By then whatever is tied up should by rights either be dead, or supporting itself.

Certain products speak of abundance, like wine, but string and twine do not. Instead, they trumpet parsimony and stinginess. Untold legions of string savers lurk among us; they only hoard, and never use. Their giant string balls grow silently, hidden away in dark cupboards. When I cut a piece of twine from the shed spool, the curse of string parsimony kicks in and the piece is invariably too short for the job, leaving me the minor humiliation of going back to cut another length to splice on to the first one. I am currently reprogramming myself to reel off the sisal like I pour the red wine.

For a time, my garden shed also housed a gasoline-powered brush saw. Built for silviculture work, I had it on temporary loan from one of my sons. I took the blade off and bought a grass whip attachment for it, which worked quite well. I soon became intrigued with the seemingly endless possibilities of my new overpowered grass whip. One pass and voila, messy garden edges were clean and straight. Weeds lurking underneath hedges were flushed out and shredded into green confetti. The lilacs, which want passionately to become full-grown trees, were now easy to top. I bought a hard hat and safety glasses, which made me look cool and professional. I was beginning to reach the top of my grass whip game, and going out of my way to find new things to shred. Fortunately, I was rescued from chronic dependence by my son, who reclaimed his brush saw, ripped the grass whip attachment off and took the machine back out to the woods where it belonged. I awoke from my petrochemical daze and realized the brush saw was not solving any garden problems, it simply made it easier to mask them.

The garden shed also houses my increasingly suspect gasoline lawn mower. As a grassland ecologist and savanna creature, I will never do away with lawns completely, but I am slowly whittling them down to pocket-sized patches that I can mow with the old-fashioned push mower of my youth, which is making a comeback.

Toad Hall

THE DOOR OF the small old-fashioned greenhouse was unlocked. The innocence of greenhouses surprises me; they are nearly always open to the casual visitor. Stepping in and closing the door firmly on a frigid winter day, I stripped off mittens, toque, scarf and overcoat, and breathed deeply. The warm, humid air was laden with the sharply contrasting odours of flowers and humus. I had come to an agricultural research station in Ottawa for a conference, and was taking a private lunchtime tour of the station's grounds when I discovered the tiny greenhouse. It was an elegant confection of plate glass and wrought iron, which made it look slightly frivolous compared to the rest of the research greenhouses, which were sleek polyethylene affairs. The sense of frivolity was reinforced when I realized this antique had no research function, but was devoted instead to the display of tropical plants. Benches crowded with potted plants lined the walls, and in the centre grew a small jungle, complete with palms, bananas and a towering *Ficus Benjamina*. A brick walkway nearly grown over with moss circled the miniature jungle. Ancient cast iron radiators clanked and hissed quietly under the benches, and from within the pocket jungle came the sound of water, dribbling down rocks into a small goldfish pond. I guessed the greenhouse dated from the very early 1900s, as it was classically Victorian in design. As a formal expression of that era's flushed and slightly breathless relationship with nature, it was perfect.

I settled into my lunchtime tour, loosening an unaccustomed tie. The little waterfall gurgled and the freighted air was rich and heady with oxygen. Leaf-shattered sunlight and the sound of running water began to have their effect, gently removing the dross of airplane travel, hotels and neon-lit conference rooms. Beyond the greenhouse's fragile curtain of glass were barren, windswept trees, dirty snowbanks and a bleak winter sky. Here inside, the environment was enfolding, almost maternal. This was the same ambience that once saved a blocked writing career. The ticking of the radiators did not measure time. As I started slowly down the brick pathway, I sensed the ancestral comfort of fertile crescents.

To tour an ornamental greenhouse is to enter the sensory regions of the brain. It is a transparent laboratory for the human response to nature, where the infinite variables of natural shape and texture, of colour and form, of temperature and humidity and light and shadow may be separated and explored. Or not separated, and explored as a simultaneous, whole experience. The greenhouse is also a kind of glass bedroom that permits a controlled intimacy with that most aloof of nature's creations, the equatorial jungle. Other creatures are often added to greenhouses, like fish, butterflies, or even birds. But the real, cosmic intent of the greenhouse is more fundamental than science, sensory stimulation or even intimacy with nature. It is a secret, reflexive closeness we seek: we enter greenhouses not so much to know nature, but to know nature in order to better understand ourselves. We enter as unknowable personae, with outward-seeing eyes, to brush pinnate palms and drooping ferns across our senses, like a newly blind man learning the lines of his own face.

The brick walkway of this Victorian miniature was only a few meters in circumference, but the greenhouse was so replete with plants that it had taken me twenty minutes to get halfway around. I inched forward, letting my eyes wander over the tangled abundance of fronds, tendrils, aerial roots and elaborate flowers. Tucked in amongst the potted plants on the benches, I noticed an ordinary potted geranium sitting on an old-fashioned balance-beam scale. Looking more closely, I saw that the balance beam was set to trip the greenhouse's automatic irrigation system as the weight of the pot decreased through water loss. This lowly geranium had been offered up as the proxy for the entire greenhouse plant community: when its roots dried to a certain point, the whole greenhouse got watered. What a lovely idea, I thought, a living ruler. Moving away from our obsession with electromechanical devices to measuring life processes with life forms. The ingenuity of the irrigation sensor was all the more compelling as it was in the service of a confection, of a non-economic frivolity. I am interested in serious frivolity, and in buildings that advertise their innocence by being unlocked.

The greenhouse dates from the early 1600s, and it originated as a creature of privilege. When tropical fruits were first brought back to Europe from the New World, the nobility determined they must have these lemons and mangoes and bananas for their tables. New World explorers like Darwin, von Humboldt and

William Bligh were charged, among other duties, with bringing seedstocks back to Europe. Castles in France, England, Italy and Germany added whole new wings, called orangeries, to grow the tender citrus and breadfruit. These orangeries had large, south-facing windows and were heated in the wintertime. In summer the trees, which were grown in large wooden tubs, were hauled outside on to an esplanade in front of the orangery. As glass became more available, orangeries evolved into greenhouses. By the mid-1800s, European fascination with New World flora had blossomed into obsession, and greenhouses evolved into palaces for the celebration of captured equatorial nature. Architects like the Englishman Decimus Burton (1800-1881) created soaring domes of glass, complete with catenary arches, ornate iron support columns, and absolutely transparent structure. Burton's Palm House, at Kew Gardens, ranks as one of the world's greatest and most recognizable buildings. The greenhouse environment was also a perfect fit with the Victorian fascination with the exotic, and the prominent sexual organs of some of the new tropical plants were no doubt a titillation.

The greenhouse I was in contained a landscape, even though it was tiny, and built from pure human artifice. As a human, I am supposed to be drawn to semi-closed landscapes, but here I was presented with two dramatic opposites — a closed-canopy jungle surrounded by a hemispheric bowl of frigid winter sky. Paradoxically, I was attracted to both.

The greenhouse is one of the lesser planets of the gardener's universe, overshadowed by ornamental gardens, domestic landscapes and public parks. The popularity of greenhouses waxes and wanes over time, but the work and dedication required to keep them running properly remains a constant.

As I continued my tour, I thought of the challenges the greenhouse landscaper faces. If one corner of a park or outdoor garden does not resonate, then the visitor can simply move to another location that does. But a greenhouse landscaper has only one chance to get it right, and this anonymous designer did it spectacularly well, leaving a small and perfect legacy of the unique Victorian fusion of architecture with nature.

The greenhouse's brick walkway looped sinuously around rockery and palm, but not artificially so, like those irritating curved walkways that take you on a circuitous route through a flat, treeless lawn. At first I concentrated on looking at the plants of the jungle to my left and the benches to my right, but then I realized there was a whole additional stratum, an understory, so to speak, of shade-loving plants growing in soil *underneath* the benches. Bent over, with hands on knees now, I retraced my steps to look at these ivies, oxalis and mosses. I have developed a state of mind which I call bemused-botanical. I didn't consciously develop it; rather it is the unintended result of years of looking at ecosystems and yards, gardens and greenhouses. The state of mind starts off by my Linnaean reflex prattling away to itself, naming the known species and wrestling with the unknowns, but then recognition lapses and conversation begins. We talk, the plants and I, about patterns, textures and communities. That conversation eventually ceases, and I slip into a primal green esthetic, driven only by the senses.

The greenhouse had me in full bemused-botanical mode as my eyes roved pleasantly across the modest profusion under the benches. My gaze was caught by a totally unexpected object. Refocussing, I realized I was looking at a huge, placid and absolutely Buddha-like toad, nestled comfortably in a bed of moss. From the size of him, I guessed this toad had been resident in the greenhouse for a number of years. Like Timothy the tortoise, he no doubt had a benefactor, probably in the form of some grizzled old technician or janitor. The toad's great cat-like eyes sparkled, and he seemed in possession of an infinite and slightly humorous wisdom.

I felt it was appropriate to acknowledge the toad somehow. Rising up and straightening my tie, I gave him a formal, Victorian bow.

Che Among the Cotoneasters

LANDSCAPE ARCHITECTURE WAS born amongst the estates and mansions of Victorian Europe, and seems inextricably bound to long, gracious sightlines, and a full-time gardening staff. There is literally nothing in the patrician history of landscape architecture that we 40x100 suburban wage slave mortals can relate to. Not yet anyway. What we need is a Leon Trotsky — nay, a Che Guevara — of landscape architecture, who can invade its aristocratic domain and pillage principles and pleasures that rightfully belong to us common folk.

The profession of landscape architecture could be said to have originated with the colourful English garden designer Lancelot Brown (1716-1783). Mr. Brown is far better known by his nickname, Capability Brown, which originated from the man's phenomenal self-promotional abilities. After visiting with a potential client, he would invariably sum up by saying, "Sir, your estate has great capability." Some of Brown's expansive garden designs are still preserved, and are considered national treasures in England.

Later on, Thomas Mawson had a seminal influence on both sides of the Atlantic. Born in Scotland in 1861, Mawson also developed prodigious talents for self-promotion and never hesitated to publicly criticize the work of predecessors like Capability Brown and Humphrey Repton. Mawson was a great advocate of formal stone terraces, complete with potted plants and statuary. In a Mawson design, one moves away from the house (read: mansion) through a series of less and less formal terraced gardens until one reaches the paddocks, which are sprinkled with picturesque highland cattle or sheep. Mawson was a master of the sight line, placing trees and other visual obstacles in such a way that the strolling garden visitor was always presented with fresh and interesting views.

Frederick Law Olmsted (1822-1903) was the first landscape architect to make an opening to ordinary people. He specialized in urban parks, and set a very high artistic bar with the grounds of the US Capitol, Chicago's Columbian Exposition, and a host of major parks in New York, Boston and elsewhere. Like other thinkers of his generation, he believed that contact with nature was essential for mental health, and that this could be achieved in cities through the provision of large urban parks. The influence of Olmsted, his sons and successors, is pervasive, stretching from Montreal to Atlanta, and from Stanford to Vancouver to Winnipeg.

I have always needed to be in the grip of some kind of adventure, be it working in South America, fighting antiwar campaigns, or exploring distant grasslands. My favourite movies involve remote locations and propeller-driven airplanes. So gardening, for me, has been a bit of a stretch. It involved some personal shifting down to a gear I probably should have been in all along. But excitement still calls. Can I push landscaping to the level of adventure? Can there be insurgency in such a staid profession? Can I boldly go forth, smashing paradigms and cotoneasters, blending nature and artifice and demanding that landscaping contribute to the eternal question of humanity's role in nature? I did find landscape adventure, curiously enough, in the works of Frederick Law Olmsted.

I carry around the notion that humans are ennobled by contact with nature. I think I got this from my mother, who was a passionate admirer of the naturalist John Muir, the man who looked at sequoias and saw cathedrals. I keep this frivolous and slightly pathetic belief mostly to myself because I am supposed to be a scientist, and the notion that we are ennobled by nature is romantic and unprovable. Ideas like that cause most scientists to break out in hives. And there is plenty of evidence to refute the idea. More and more, we live in glass-walled cities, and yet we do great and wonderful things from within them.

I keep at my bedside a few books by writers who speak unabashedly of the process of nature ennoblement, like Muir, Walt Whitman, Loren Eiseley, Barry Lopez and others. They allow me to sustain our fragile and jointly held secret. Olmsted's writings arrived like a bombshell, opening up this exclusive and slightly sanctimonious club. Here was an individual who was practical, successful, and urban, and yet he embraced the ennoblement idea. And not just for the select few, but for the masses. In fact, the ennoblement process motivated his life's work in designing urban parks. Here is a fragment from his writings:

"It is a scientific fact that the occasional contemplation of natural scenes of an impressive character . . . is favourable to the health and vigor of men and especially to the health and vigor of their intellect . . . "

And further:

"It [the contemplation of nature] is for itself and at the moment that it is enjoyed. The attention is aroused and the mind occupied without purpose, without a continuation of the common process of relating the present action, thought or perception to some future end. There is little else that has this quality so purely."

Clearly, this was a man who understood the bemused-botanical state of mind.

Olmsted was highly successful in convincing government authorities that setting aside large tracts of land for urban parks was not only their duty, but in their economic self-interest, because urban workers with easy access to nature would be happier and more productive.

Gardens are diminutive parks, I reckon, so the Olmsted ennoblement mechanism should be at work in both. Thanks to the dashing Frederick I can bring ennoblement out of the closet, and that is thrilling, that is adventure right in my own garden.

Going out on a metaphorical limb here, I see a kind of genetic rationale for what Olmsted, Muir, and even the horticultural therapists propose, and the logic goes something like this: we humans evolved with nature, in the landscape. As a result, we have ingrained responses to nature and landscape that are adaptive and valuable for us as a species. However these organismic reactions are instinctive, lying mostly below the level of consciousness. Explosive technological progress has distanced us from these ancient responses, which are subtle at the best of times. So we need to preserve some last shards of undisturbed natural landscapes, and go back out to them periodically. Once there, in nature, we can engage all our senses to identify those forgotten responses, and to understand the particular config-urations of landscape, vegetation and biota that trigger them. To find out why rocks emanate timelessness, why sunflowers code for optimism, and grasslands speak of freedom. Then we need to bring that recovered understanding back to the city, and recreate those configurations in miniature. Most of us don't have the opportunity for daily contact with nature, but we can interact frequently with urban yards, gardens, parks and boulevards, so these can be proxies in the process of re-weaving nature back into our culture and our daily lives.

The re-weaving is a long-term project requiring many trades and apprenticeships. On the nature side, there are jobs for environmentalists, to preserve those remaining shards of nature from development. Those who prefer the ecological restoration path can rebuild examples of damaged or extirpated landscapes. There is work for ecologists, in helping both groups define and understand healthy natural landscapes. On the yard and garden side, there is work for the permaculturist, the landscaper, the botanist, the horticultural therapist. And in recapturing our timeless understandings of nature and bringing them home to our gardens, there is work for everyone.

Rituals, particularly those that connect humans to nature, have played a crucial role in human societies over time. Our contemporary society, for a host of reasons, has few meaningful rituals. Eco-philosopher, William Jordan, thinks that the activity of ecological restoration presents the opportunity to create new and profound rituals based on respect for nature, the understanding of its workings, and the activities of healing damaged pieces of it. I'd like to go one better, and suggest that some of these new nature-culture rituals could also embrace yards, gardens and parks.

As an ecologist, I am constantly confronted with nature's ironies, conundrums, and paradoxes. A rare plant species is found growing on mine tailings. The sharptail grouse likes heavily overgrazed pastures for its mating dance leks. Natural disturbances can be good and bad at the same time: too much fire is destructive, so is too little. And one of my favourites: great efforts were expended to reintroduce the rare burrowing owl in the BC Interior, but then biologists discovered that the ungrateful owls were feasting on the treasured and iconic western bluebirds. The human mind needs to confront nature, because nature asks good, hard questions.

Christopher Alexander is a contemporary architect who has made significant contributions to the democratization of landscape architecture. In his seminal work, A *Pattern Language*, he recognizes the continuum between the elements of interior design, architecture, landscape architecture and urban planning, and describes timeless examples from each discipline. I am sure there must have been some drudgery associated with the massive compilation that is A *Pattern Language*, but then think of the joys of searching the world over for the best possible example of say, an arbour, or a garden path.

I pick up A *Pattern Language* often, and it helps to remind me that the ill-conceived walkways and terraces I wrestle with *are* elements that have already been defined — and wrestled with — for centuries. But one cannot create a pleasing yard by simply adding a bunch of elements — a planter here, a hedge there, a walkway somewhere else. Like a sentence with no verbs, that kind of landscaping lacks flow, continuity and linkage. Defining and creating a landscape element is the easy part. Joining that element in harmony with other garden elements is the bigger challenge. I am currently planning a stretch of drypointed rock wall that ends in a short stairway leading from one terrace level to another. I have built both rock walls and stairways before, but this time my planning (more precisely, the idle musing I do while throwing sticks for Spud) is focussed on how to bring those two elements gracefully together. Rock walls must bond to their stairways, just as gardens must bond to nature.

It is no wonder that landscape architecture has no currency for the average person. The discipline has gone from serving the estates of the idle rich to being the complacent lapdog of corporate high rise and big box architecture, where a lonely strip of bedraggled cotoneaster drowning in bark mulch and surrounded by vast tectonic plates of concrete is called "landscaping." Corporate views of landscape architecture often approximate S&M: the emphasis is on restraint. Some examples are so bad they literally suck the oxygen from the streetscape.

One of the hallmarks of corporate and subdivision landscape architecture is that it is designed not to evolve. The isolated shrubs and single specimen trees and geometric lawns will look the same in ten years as they do now, and the buildings they are designed to complement will still look just as disconnected from the neighbourhood and the earth — as if they accidentally fell off the loading dock of some giant prefab factory in space.

When a new and unwanted commercial development goes into a neighbourhood, landscape architects are invariably brought in to soften the blow of the megamall or highrise tower. And then suddenly, a curious thing happens: we go mute. If a trained professional is telling us the landscaping is esthetically pleasing, ties the structure to the site and softens the angularity, when all we see is the cotoneaster-and-bark-mulch disaster, then we obviously just don't understand. So we tend to think there is something mysterious and complicated about landscape architecture, which we can't see with our untrained eyes.

Not true.

Most people would never dream of dignifying their humble yard and garden work by calling it landscape architecture, but that in fact is what it is. We create assemblages, we mix colours and seasons of colour, we contrast textures, we soften hard edges and build structures with plantings, we anchor our homes to the lot, and apartment balconies to the earth. There are a couple of objective principles to landscape architecture, borrowed mostly from art, that deal with perspective, complementarity and harmony. Then there is the matter of plant requirements and adaptation, knowledge simply borrowed from the disciplines of horticulture and arboriculture. And like the ecologist, the landscape architect must have an empathy for plants and the patience to learn how they relate to each other in groups. Add in a basic understanding of human behavior and perception, and that's it. Beyond that, the rest of landscape architecture is as subjective as art, and as capricious as fashion. So it is a discipline open to all of us, demanding only simple engagement and sustained attention.

One of the biggest challenges in domestic landscape architecture is to link plantings together in a natural and pleasing way. Economics is an issue here; instead of buying five or fifteen plants of a kind to create the more natural massed plantings, we tend to be conservative and buy one or two of a species, to plant them as "specimens." I am guilty of this sin, except I tend to buy two of everything, just in case one dies. Two of everything looks just as dumb as one of everything. Specimen planting only works in contrast to an adjacent massed planting. A yard full of "specimens" makes neither ecological nor esthetic sense.

Serendipity and personal meaning should play a major role in landscaping, as it certainly has in mine. Some years ago we were visiting Vancouver's famed Van Dusen Gardens. It was a fall family outing, and I had on my father's old Harris Tweed jacket, which I save for occasions. We passed a bare tree that had a single, odd-shaped fruit left hanging on it. I reached over and feloniously picked the fruit, noting as I did so the tree's nameplate: medlar (*Mespilus germanica*), a member of the apple subfamily. The fruit was about the size and shape of a garlic bulb, with a fringed opening at the bottom. I made a mental note to look into this odd tree but of course promptly forgot about it.

A month later I had occasion to put on the Harris Tweed again, and felt something in the side pocket. I reached in and retrieved the forgotten medlar fruit, now gone all soft and squishy. Since it was part of the apple family, I tempted a bite. The dark brown flesh was the colour and consistency of a ripe fig, and tasted like applesauce. I was intrigued, and looked up the medlar. It turns out that the medlar was a popular fruit in Medieval Europe, but was eclipsed by other fruits and eventually forgotten. Predictably, the medlar carries with it a raft of folkloric baggage, most of it bawdy, since the bottom of the fruit bears some resemblance to the human posterior. The medlar fruit, I read, requires a month of afterripening (other authors called it "rotting") before it is edible. By sheer incompetent fluke, I had precisely replicated the medlar "bletting" (an old English word for afterripening) process in the pocket of my father's coat. Naturally I went on a quest for a medlar tree, and secured one from Chilliwack's gardening genius, Brian Minter. So full-on, funky serendipity has placed a medlar in my front yard, not far from Percy Wright's Yellow Altai rose. A personal connection, or even just a good story, is reason enough for me to violate my rule about single, "specimen plantings".

Landscape architecture has yet to make the transition from the grandiose to the suburban lot, like ecology has. Some ecologists specialize in landscape ecology, others like myself in the more localized and small-scale community ecology. Community ecology requires us to focus our attention to the middle distance, using what I call the "short eye". The short eye works against the grain of the human psyche, which is naturally attracted to long vistas, ones we can see from atop mountains and from other strategic view locations. When we arrive at a new place, our eyes automatically seek the horizon. "View lots" that look out on distant views of mountains, lakes or oceans always have a real estate premium attached, because we crave that long view. We tend to scan the perimeter, not the core. Community-level ecologists like myself attempt to suppress that natural impulse, and shorten our focus to key on that zone between the close-up and the long vista. In the course of my grassland field work, when I come into a new area, I resist the temptation to focus immediately either on the distance, or on the plants directly in front of me. I have trained myself to do a methodical scan of the nearby, middle-distance terrain first, looking for slope breaks, wet spots or subtle changes in soil texture that might help define the boundaries of the plant community (the ecological neighbourhood) I am in. Once those boundaries are fixed in my mind, then I can begin to look at the community in front of me. Once I get a sense of the dominant species, then I let my calibrated eye wander back out, to see if I've drawn the boundaries right.

The ecological short eye (actually, a "medium eye"), and the habit of mentally tracing in those intimate polygons of native plant communities, turns out to be a good basis for domestic landscape architecture. The habit adapts well to our suburban yards. They help me look at my garden, which is tightly circumscribed by curb, fence and alley, as a small but sufficient universe.

One of the keys to the gardening short eye is to substitute complexity for distance. By building layers, gradations, interruptions and switchbacks, the gardener creates a landscape of visual density and possibility, a yard in which you can take a twenty-minute walk and not leave home. Think of domestic, 40x100 landscaping as an exercise in Hobbitization.

Looming in the background of landscape architecture is the awful question of the lawn. A traditional favourite for parks and homes, the omnipresent flat lawn has recently come under intense criticism. It is seen as a monoculture, an energy pig, an English colonial anachronism, a chemical addict and an environmental suspect. I will add another personal complaint to this list: a flat, featureless lawn is an esthetic zero. It is the sightline, without the sight. I further dislike lawns because they harken back to the stately days in Europe when the grand manor loomed above acres of manicured and leisurely grass. My ancestors did not participate in this manorial tradition; they probably lived in the grimy hovels around back. I can carry a grudge for a long time.

A student of the lawn must turn to anthropology to explain its pervasiveness. One writer suggested the lawn is a means of flaunting one's wealth. The grassy expanse trumpets the fact that the owner is so wealthy he can devote productive land to useless ornamentation instead of using it for food crops or a livestock pasture. This might seem a very primitive motivation, until one looks at women's fashion magazines, which are about as current as you can get. One of the plausible explanations for the bizarre obsession with thinness in women's fashion is that it also trumpets wealth. The skinny body image says "look at me, I live in such an affluent milieu that I don't need stored fat to survive. Food will always be available for me."

When we lived in one of the prairie cities, we had a very practical Ukrainian neighbour who devoted his entire front yard to potatoes. Others on our city block were offended, and looked for bylaws that might prohibit front yard potato production. Compared to their underutilized and overwatered lawns though, I thought the neatly arranged hills and lush potato foliage made a nice esthetic statement.

The lawn is often the whitebread, dumbed-down, token solution for a lack of genuine interest in plants and landscaping. A painter approaches a blank canvas with a mixture of passion and trepidation; as we democratize and re-invent domestic landscape architecture, lawns should inspire us in the same way.

Another awful question facing landscape architecture is the automobile, and its sprawling paraphernalia of highways, roads, alleys, parking lots, parkades and garages. It is interesting to reflect on just how rapidly the automobile became a dominant consideration in landscape architecture. Even Thomas Mawson, the champion of the house and yard as a single esthetic statement, incorporated the newly-arrived motorcar in his later designs. The car now rules the house, just as its associated concrete paraphernalia rule our cities.

One of my own landscaping considerations is age, which the lawn also bears upon. Sidling into my sixties, still waiting to see how I turn out, I know there will come a time when I am no longer be able to drag my 22-inch gas powered lawn mower around. Upon reaching that male watershed, the traditional thing to do is to hire the thirteen-year old neighbour kid to mow the lawn for you. However, having been that neighbour kid myself once, working under the hypercritical gazes of several old farts who had mowed to their own exacting standards for decades and then could no longer do it but nonetheless missed the private male satisfactions of lawnmowing terribly, I know that hiring a kid will not work for me either. While I still can, I need to push my yard toward a fine-grained, metastable savanna mosaic of garden beds, solid stone walls, gentle pathways and small grassed areas that I can chip away at with a heritage push mower. Or use my senior citizen status to argue for an exemption to the City's Livestock Bylaw, and get a sheep.

Building a garden is a bit like building your own house while you live in it. Every flaw, every unfinished bit is a constant nagging presence, and the process of mental redesign goes on continuously. Sometimes I look at what I have created and see nothing but chaos, which is probably what the neighbours see as well. But then I remind myself of the recent connection between chaos and ecology. The new theorists of chaos have made their presence felt in ecology, and in a host of other disciplines. They avow that nature actually likes a certain amount of random confusion. They say that if an ecosystem has the opportunity to choose where it positions itself along a continuum that starts with a single-species monoculture and ends in a chaotically random assortment of vegetation, that the ecosystem will actually gravitate to a little beyond the midpoint, on the chaotic side of things. Even though I hate the math the chaos types always indulge in, their theory fits my garden, and my lifestyle. A little bit of chaos is good.

Ecology tries desperately to be a hard science like physics, but the core of ecology is romantic in the best sense. Ecologists believe a community of species is more than just a sum of its parts. They see a "group mind" where the accumulated genetic wisdom of individual species is complemented by a community wisdom — where species come together in reciprocating, repeatable and intelligent groupings. When I look out at my garden, I see a similar process, where the laborious addition of plants, rock walls and compost will someday coalesce into an aesthetic as well as a biological whole.

Ecology is not only romantic, it is an integrative discipline, which puts it at odds with the rest of science. Ecologist Vladimir Krajina, who fled from Czechoslovakia to British Columbia in 1949, was an integrator par excellence. After studying BC's ecosystems for a couple of decades, he devised an ecological classification framework known as the "biogeoclimatic" system. Not a phrase that rolls off the tongue easily, "biogeoclimatic" recognizes the three great kings of ecology: biology, geology, and climate. The interaction of these three regal forces produces local ecosystems. We can use the biogeoclimatic concept to our advantage in making our gardening and landscaping more locally adapted, but first we must acknowledge the fourth king, that of culture. Vladimir did well collapsing three disparate concepts into a single term, now part of British Columbia's natural lexicon. I'm not sure "biogeoculturoclimatic" will catch on to the same degree. Maybe I'll have to be content with "the whole enchilada".

By placing yard and garden art, we are practicing the essence of landscape architecture, which is the graceful integration of built structures with vegetation, of culture with nature. Again, most of us would never dream of dignifying our humble yard and garden activities with so noble a term, but landscape architecture is in fact what we are doing when we create assemblages, soften hard edges with plantings and bring in that ubiquitous concrete frog. Domestic landscape architecture is about anchoring our homes and our experiences and our desires in a landscape.

Landscape architecture also serves the split Eden. Two of my neighbours, whose houses face each other, approach landscaping from perspectives that could not be more different. Fred, the neighbour to the south, lines his flowerbeds with concrete and favours bright bunches of fertilizer-enhanced annuals. He placed his two pyramidal cedars in the front yard with geometric precision. The square lawn is always green and evenly mowed. Fred prides himself on his vegetable forcing skills; his tomatoes are the earliest and biggest in the neighbourhood. Damian, directly across the street from Fred, has an unmowed front yard and an elaborate kitchen garden full of European herbs.

His back garden is a veritable cathedral to the organic. As for trees, he has planted native saskatoons and birches. I have never seen the two neighbours speak to each other, which is really not surprising, but I enjoy the company, and the gardening enthusiasm, of both. It is good to be surrounded by other lives, and other yards. Each one is different, but the evening breeze stirs them all.

An indigenous landscape architecture, based on north American climates and vegetation, designed for the suburban lot that is 50% occupied by a house, and that acknowledges the time and financial pressures of the two-breadwinner household, and that resonates with nature, has yet to be created. It still awaits its Che Guevara. Maybe that will be me, when I can't mow the lawn anymore.

THE CLIMATE OF THE KETTLE

FOR SEVERAL YEARS now, I have looked after a small remote weather station, at one of my long-term grassland research sites. Twice a year I make the drive up a steep access road to the station, situated on a grassy bench overlooking the valley of the Kettle River, a tributary of the Columbia. The weather recording apparatus is somewhat fantastical, and looks like a primitive, malnourished cyborg. What passes for the beast's head is a small inclined solar panel; one outstretched arm holds the wind direction and temperature gauge, while the other holds aloft the windspeed rotor. The single eyeball is the radiometer, which tracks the amount of sunshine. The stomach is a square metal box containing the electronic datalogger which digests the weather data, the backbone is the aluminium pole everything is attached to, and the tripod base passes for legs. The weather station is held captive inside a small exclosure of sagging woven wire, so the overall impression is that of a rural robot zoo that has fallen on hard times.

The station's data logger is truly ancient; in order to download the weather data from it I have to bring along an equally ancient laptop, and remember all my DOS commands (weather geeks seem to be militantly attached to pre-Windows environments). Once I get the laptop connected, everything set up, and the precise keystrokes entered, six months worth of Kettle Valley weather — in fifteen minute increments — flows quietly into the laptop. As I wait for this mysterious process to complete, I sit in the short grass and look at my binder full of weather data. From this site I can just see the village of Midway down in the valley, probably less than three kilometres distant. Somehow, the climate at Midway's weather station is subtly and marvellously different from the climate here. And the weather this year on this Kettle Valley grassland will be subtly and marvellously different from the weather next year. And the vegetation here and in Midway, this year and next year, will also be subtly different.

Spring is the crucial season for plants in nature as well as the garden, but as I look over my weather data book, I am struck by how no two springs are ever completely alike. I am tremendously impressed by people who can remember these sequences, who can tell you what spring was like ten years ago. I myself need binders full of data.

The sequence and interplay of temperature, precipitation, humidity, wind, and hours of sunshine varies almost infinitely, and the plants I sit on are infinitely exposed to this variation. The bunchgrass, sticky geranium, phlox, and the rest of the plants of this grassland suite — including the ever present Kentucky bluegrass — must either adapt to this variation, or die.

One of the aspects of wild nature that so fascinates me is its complete indifference to individual lives.

Gardens are vastly different environments. In gardens we actively intervene on behalf of individual plants, and we modify climate to suit them. In fact, whatever the local climate is, we generally work against it in our yards and gardens. We grow English lawns in the desert, and force tomatoes in the Yukon. We create raised beds in rainforest climates, to dry out the soil. We change the aspect, from north-facing to level, or from level to south-facing. We plant close to buildings which trap and reradiate solar heat, and screen plants from desiccating winds. We apply insulating mulch in the winter, we fertilize to kick-start growth in the spring, and we water through the dry spells. We even put water-filled plastic jackets around our spring tomatoes. In other words, we gardeners are forever pushing in the opposite direction of the prevailing climate. But in the end, climate defines the look of our gardens, and the suite of plants available to us. At 300 millimeters of precipitation per year, both ecosystems and landscaping tend toward openness, with scattered trees and low-growing, durable plants. At 600 millimeters, growth can be denser, taller and more delicate.

The common mugho pine is a good bellwether of the regional climate. On the Canadian prairies it is a compact, ground-hugging shrub, rarely venturing its stems more than a meter high. Annual growth can be measured in millimetres. It thrives in the wet areas of British Columbia, each spring putting up finger-sized candles of new growth. Unless the gardener is vigilant in trimming the candles, a British Columbia mugho soon becomes a leggy and grotesque tree.

I always enjoy driving through mountain passes because they are ecological transitions. In the space of an hour or two, you can do an ecological tour from valley bottom to alpine and back again. The lowland ecosystem on one side of a major mountain chain is never replicated on the other side, even when you return to the same elevation. Rain shadows, wind patterns, temperature ranges and a dozen other forces all conspire to create subtle differences. Going from the prairies through the Rockies into the intermountain valleys of the West is a profound ecological transition, as is the next westerly hurdle, over the Cascade/Coast Mountains into the lowlands of the Pacific. When I went on family road trips as a child, I delighted in sticking my hand out the car window and cupping it into an airfoil, to feel the tug and lift of wind on my skin. I still let my hand fly on occasion, but now my favourite road trip diversion is a visual one, watching the subtle weave of ecosystems as they pass by.

As a high school kid, I used to indulge in a Saturday night activity we blatantly called the Chinese fire drill. A bunch of testosterone-fuelled buddies in a battered old four-door, we would pull up to a stoplight, throw open the doors, and everyone would jump out and quickly change positions. At the next stoplight, we would change back, and so on. The frenetic uselessness of the activity appealed to all of us. Every spring I do something akin to the Chinese fire drill in my garden. I put a plant in, give it a year or maybe two at the most, and if it isn't doing well, I'll dig it up and move it somewhere else. There is no real logic to this activity, other than the fact that it occasionally works. But spending time with the Kettle River weather data has made me think in terms of microclimates, of the bubble of actual weather conditions right around the individual plant, how important that is, and how different it can be from one side of the valley to the other, from one side of the yard to the other. So when

I move a plant, there's a reasonable chance the new location will have a microclimate that is different and better than the previous one, rather than different and worse.

An entomologist acquaintance was studying foraging spiders that inhabited unstable sand dunes in Namibia. He was intrigued by their ability to range widely across the featureless and shifting sand, yet always return to their subterranean burrows at the end of the day. After much study, the entomologist concluded the spiders' outstanding navigational ability was based on fuzzy logic. In other words, an enhanced and systematized version of trial and error. That's what I'm doing when I move plants around the yard.

Canadian gardeners as well as those in the northern tier of US states all pay homage to the south aspect, orienting their plantings in that direction to maximize sunshine, and lengthen the season. However, there is a subtle distinction between south, and southwest. As a grassland ecologist, I bow specifically to the southwest, not from geodetic idiosyncrasy, but because that is the warmest aspect of the compass rose. You might argue that the maximum hours of sun exposure would be captured by a direct south aspect, which is true. If you were putting up a solar panel, which is indifferent to temperature, you would orient it due south. But if you have the choice of aspects when designing a northern garden, you choose a southwest orientation, because of an eco-physiological peculiarity, which goes like this. Most plants do not, physiologically, "open for business" until the air temperature hits about ten degrees Celsius. In the shoulder seasons of spring and fall, mornings are often too cold for plant growth, so the early, easterly sun is wasted, so to speak. But once the sun has warmed the air to that magic ten degree threshold for biological activity, plants on the southwest aspect get the longest dalliance in the afternoon sun. As a result, southwest has slightly less hours of sunlight than a pure south aspect, but a considerably longer growing season.

The southwest aspect can sometimes be a liability, since the longer growing season can produce drought stress. In the mountains, steep southwest aspects are typically grasslands or shrublands, since these slopes dry out too much to support trees. In gardens, southwest sunshine in the early spring can trigger sunscald in evergreens. Sunscald is actually a misnomer, since the true culprit is not sun, but water. When spring air warms up enough for conifers to open their stomates and start photosynthesis, but the ground is still frozen, it means the tree or shrub is demanding water but can't get any. Needles and sometimes whole branches die as a result, nearly always on the southwest side of the tree. Deciduous shrubs and trees neatly bypass this problem by having no active leaf area during the tricky season of early spring.

Every region has its own particular climatic challenge; here it is snowpress. I can recite a litany of plants I have lost to it. A young Gala apple, in its first year of bearing fruit, snapped off right at the basal graft by a wet October snow. A rhododendron crushed by massive furrows thrown up over the curb by the city's snowplow. An azalea taken down by a spring ice crust. A pyramidal cedar in the side yard survives the snowpress, but if I don't tie it up every winter, snow accumulates and forces the upper branches outward until the cedar resembles a bizarre northern palm tree. Every fall I stubbornly refuse to tie it up, vowing any plant that can't face the elements on it's own doesn't belong in my yard. But by Christmas, I relent. That wussiness

DON GAYTON

condemns me to the gardening minors, rather than playing in the big leagues along with mother nature.

Adapted plants resist snowpress by either being very stiff, very narrow or very flexible. Western red cedar is the ultimate practitioner of the flexible strategy. Cedar branch wood is sprung into a graceful arc that sweeps downward away from the trunk, and towards the tip it flares upward again, anticipating snowload. On a warming day after a heavy snowfall, a cedar forest is alive with swishing sounds and motions as, one by one, heavily laden branches slip their loads and swing back up to their original position.

Along with cedar, yew is also native to this heavy snowfall region, and I planted one in my yard. When it got caught and badly deformed by snowpress I was surprised, since I assumed it would be immune. Then I thought about the yew's niche in nature. This large shrub/small tree is a forest *understory* species, content to grow in perpetual shade, leaving the big cedars and firs above it to carry the brunt of the snowload. I had unthinkingly planted it right out in the open. As a landscaper, I seem to suffer from ecological disconnect: my impetuous horticultural miscues are explained by sober ecological second thoughts.

Most of our contact with climate information, as opposed to weather reports, is boiled down to that brief exchange at our local nursery, when we ask if plant X is hardy where we live. I honestly don't know the precise hardiness zone my yard is in, but I have an excuse, since mountainous areas like the one I live in are a nightmare for the scientists that do hardiness zone mapping. Satellite photos of this region are strongly reminiscent of the reticulated surface of the brain, with complex ranges and

~ 118 ~

tortuous valleys running off in every compass direction. With continuously changing aspect and elevation, it is no wonder montane regions are such a joy to explore and such a challenge to map.

The original hardiness zone maps, still in use in the United States, are based on the average temperatures of the coldest winter month, but plant hardiness is far more complex than that. The recently revised Canadian system incorporates a basket of parameters, including the mean minimum temperature of the coldest month, the maximum for the warmest month, the length of the frost-free period, summer rainfall amounts, maximum windspeed, and elevation. The Canadian mappers integrated this great mass of data using a thin-plate smoothing spline, which is not something you would pick up at a transmission repair shop, but is actually a statistical tool. Even with this level of sophistication though, the Canadian mappers put a disclaimer on their mountain data.

Plant hardiness zones represent our crude attempts to view the world through the senses of a plant. The Canadian scientists have also tagged a common shrub that is emblematic of each of their nine zones: if you live in zone 0, in northern Canada, you can grow the Labrador tea shrub with confidence. If you are in the mildest zone, 8, you can probably grow all the previous zones' shrubs, and spotted laurel as well.

To call someone who studies mosses a half-mad bryologist is probably redundant, but I have a friend, Terry, who is one. I once spent three days with him, walking the shores of muddy sloughs in November, looking for a red-listed moss, *Pterygonerum kozlovii*. (As my father used to say, the "P" is silent, like in swimming.) Bryologists are so exclusive that they often disdain common names; *Pterygonerum* doesn't really have one. After much looking, Terry did finally find his moss, and he was ecstatic as he pointed out the subminute features that distinguished *Pterygonerum* from all the other scruffy little mosses around the edge of the stagnant slough. I looked around the muddy expanse we were in, and then I looked at the low clouds overhead threatening snow, then I looked at Terry, and finally, I looked at his precious moss.

It might be red-listed, but it still looks like frog spit to me, I said.

In order to repair our friendship, I thought I would start a moss garden. I had the perfect place for it. The narrow space between my house and the neighbour's was partly occupied by my downscale tool shed, but the lower part was essentially vacant, except for a flagrantly disobedient honeysuckle. The soil in this space was terrible and filled with broken concrete, so a moss planting seemed like the way to go. The long, narrow space got maybe forty-five minutes of direct sun exposure, and for the rest of the day it experienced subdued and reflected light. Nearby fences and house walls would block the wind and trap humidity, I thought. A few mosses do grow around muddy sloughs, but most of them like a nice shady forest floor environment, which I could recreate. I consulted on the moss garden with Terry, who was on speaking terms with me again.

Don't bring the moss, bring the rock the moss is growing on, he said. This severely limited my options, and made me wonder if this was a form of retribution, but I did as I was told, and made an artistic arrangement with stones hosting some common but elegant sphagnum, hylocomium and dicranium mosses.

Within a few weeks my mosses had all shrivelled to a dull, grey crust. Sitting in my failed shady forest glen moss garden, I speculated on the reasons for its failure. It couldn't be water, since I had been conscientious about spraying them lightly every two or three days. It couldn't be nutrients, because mosses don't need much, and when they first arrived I had spritzed them with a very weak fertilizer solution. I had specifically chosen mosses from sites that got about the same amount of sun as my shady forest glen site. So the only variable left, short of some poetic dying of a broken heart, was humidity. I borrowed a relative humidity meter and checked a sunny part of the front yard, as a benchmark, and then went into my shady forest glen to take another reading. Both readings were identical, and quite low. So my shady forest glen was missing that defining characteristic of a real wet forest — humid air, which is essential for rootless mosses. Apparently vinyl siding and wooden fencing were no match for the moisture-holding capacities of shaggy cedar trunks and drooping branches. I'm sure Terry could have forewarned me about humidity, had he been so inclined.

The shady forest glen moss garden project is on hold for now, until I figure out a way to generate humid air without rotting adjacent fences and houses.

We are profoundly conscious of weather, but in a highly subjective way. Our range of acceptable conditions is fairly broad during the week, but narrows dramatically on weekends. Our perception of how cold, hot, wet or windy it is depends very much on what we are doing, what we are wearing, where we were raised, and whether we ski or sail. Our garden plants do not have the luxury of subjectivity, clothing or movement. After my moss garden debacle, I vowed to pay more attention to garden microclimates as a gesture of vegetable respect. A First Nations colleague of mine, who does prescribed burns to thin the dry forests on his Reserve, suggested I try a trick of his. Atmospheric humidity levels are crucial in planning prescribed burns, and he was developing an intuitive sense of humidity by comparing the instrument readings to a series of sensations — how the air felt against his skin, how crunchy the duff layer was, and how loudly a dry twig sounded when he broke it.

Climatically, I live in a hinged ecosystem, as do many who live in North America's intermountain West. There is plenty of rain to encourage forest trees but the hot, dry summers do stress the trees, leaving the field open for grasses and shrubs. I am temperamentally better suited to the grassland side of the hinge, so when I look out our bedroom window and see the gargantuan balsam fir, it is an affront. The tree's form, colour, growth rate and even smell are emblematic of wet forest, of grassland antithesis. The tree continuously replaces its shiny foliage, so drifts of shed needles accumulate in the rain gutters. It blocks the view from our bedroom window, demanding that I look at it instead of the scenery behind it. Every spring a pair of Steller's bluejays inspect the tree closely, debating its merits as a nest site, and then move on. In late summer the tree exudes a fine, sticky rain of sap, which attracts legions of hornets and yellowjackets. The balsam fir is totally unsuitable as a landscape tree. I am sure, somewhere in its coniferous consciousness, that the tree considers me and my house as a totally unsuitable nuisance that has been tolerated long enough. In some future epoch when it finally falls down, it will take out half the neighbourhood. My balsam fir is not a tree, it is an event, and my pathetic attempts to control it have been futile. But it is wonderfully adapted to the particular microclimate of our backyard and serves to remind me that in spite of my grassland temperament, I live for now on the forest side of the climate hinge.

Consider the Lilacs

GARDENS LIKE MINE are chattels, bound by the strange phenomenon of private land ownership. My experience of the garden is largely exclusive, and private. I take solitary pleasure in working with my own plants, using my own tools and making unilateral garden decisions, without consultation. As I lean on rake or shovel, not doing anything in particular except enjoying the garden's burgeoning presence, I am conscious of a kind of selfish privilege. There is some show involved; I like to have passersby admire it and visitors to enjoy it, but fundamentally, the garden is for me. So that makes it suspect.

Fortunately, lilacs are there to remind me there is no such thing as a truly private garden. My lilacs, or rather, the people's lilacs that happen to grow in my yard, form a tall hedge along the street. When they bloom, everyone from pre-schoolers to senior citizens help themselves to the flowers. Like pumpkins, they seem to be owned in common. Strangers who are otherwise absolutely respectful of private property, somehow intuitively know it is okay to come into someone's yard to collect a spray of the wonderfully scented purple blooms. The lilacs themselves encourage this floral socialism by being so utterly profligate in their beauty. I have encouraged it too, by pruning and mulching the hedge.

When we bought the place, the lilacs had been neglected for years, and the hedge had become an unpleasant row of spindly, tree-sized lilacs with a few pathetic blooms up high, a few starving suckers underneath. Before I could do anything with them, I first had to convince my wife that cutting the massive stems right back to the ground was a good thing, which would give the hedge a new lease on life. Based on some of my previous exploits, that was a tough sell, but finally successful. I started with the Swede saw, but was stunned by the ebony-like hardness of the wood. So I defaulted on my manual tradition, and enlisted one of my sons to do the chainsaw work.

The pruned lilacs responded beautifully, producing a thick, head-high forest of fresh new stems in the first season. The second year after renovation they bloomed profusely, much to the delight of passersby. However, the lilacs still harbour a burning desire to become trees, so I have to top them regularly.

My lilacs are the traditional *Syringa vulgaris* type, the utterly common suckering variety, which is probably the earliest, most widespread and most durable introduced ornamental in the New World. Virtually every schoolhouse and farmyard, from northern Canada to Colorado, has a lilac. The common lilac has also become the gold standard for plant phenological studies. Since it is so uniform and so widespread, the date that it flowers is used as a common measure for springtime weather conditions. As this lilac data slowly accumulates, it can be used as a graphic, real-time measure of climate change.

The original lilacs grew wild in the Carpathian Mountains of Romania, but it was the French horticulturists that shaped it into the plant we know today. Once established in the New World, it was fiercely adopted by various individuals, including a couple of early American farmers by the names of Washington and Jefferson. Regions adopted it too, such as New Hampshire, which designated it as their State Flower. But nineteenth-century Canada literally embraced the lilac, making it an integral part of their westward expansion. The cold but fertile regions of the prairies and the Rockies were promoted as literal gardens for the immigrant farmer, and the lilac would be there to help domesticate the wilderness, and bring the solace of floral beauty to the homesteader's wife. The flat, windy Canadian prairies offered few inviting spots for homestead sites, so the development of windbreaks was crucial. There are precious few plant species that can stand unprotected in the rigours of a Canadian prairie winter and still make an effective windbreak. Right at the top of that very, very short list, along with the caragana and the Siberian elm, is the common lilac. Early Irish immigrants to Canada brought their own lilac slips with them, keeping the cuttings moist between the halves of a split potato.

When we lived on the prairies, we had a neighbour who nursed an enduring love for his four-wheel drive truck and an enduring hatred for an old bull lilac bush in his front yard. One spring these two passions collided, when Al decided to get rid of the lilac. After digging mightily for several hours, he had exposed some of the plant's octopus-like roots, but it wouldn't budge. In an outpouring of syringiac rage, he backed his truck up onto the lawn and wrapped a tow chain around the base of the lilac. After several unsuccessful pulls, Al backed his truck right up against the lilac, and floored it to get a running start. The impact shook the neighbourhood, but only caused a few small roots to snap. The lilac was steadfast, and Al's truck went in for a costly bent frame repair.

My lilacs consort happily with perennial sweetpea, another European ornamental that probably came to this country about the same time as the lilac. The perennial sweetpea jumps the garden fence occasionally, but in a non-weedy sort of way. When one showed up in my lilac hedge, I made sure it felt right at home. Using its tendrils, the sweetpea rappelled its curious winged stems up through the lilac branches to sunlight. In the fall, I collected the tightly coiled seedpods just before they exploded, and scattered the seed through the rest of the hedge. Now the lilacs get the benefit of the sweetpea's leguminous nitrogen, and I get the benefit of a second set of pickable purple flowers, a few weeks after the lilacs have finished.

Perhaps the lilac's success, its role in westward expansion, and the ease of propagating it has contributed to its identity as a public plant, owned by everyone. The other plant universally recognized as common property is the apple tree. The generous, half-wild quality of the lilac and the apple and the sweetpea sets them both apart from other, more private plants.

Even though I can produce title to this scrap of urban land, gardens cannot really be owned in the same way a car or a boat can be. A garden is a gift, a celebration, and a revelation. And all gardens are partly owned by nature, which makes unilateral decisions of her own occasionally, in the form of heavy, wet snowfalls or three weeks in July without rain.

Evening is my favourite time in the yard. Temperatures cool off, and the wars of the day are all done. I can stand with the garden hose, nozzle set to a coarse mist, perhaps a glass of wine in hand, and offer random comfort. The dog snuffles about, searching for some nameless canine mystery under the mugho pines. It is a good time to think about succession, in a personal sense. My early seral starting point was probably around age twelve, when our family moved to the country. The house had a few acres attached to it, and the previous owner had tried a market garden and failed, leaving behind a large plot of asparagus to go feral. I prowled amongst the great bushy rows of bolted asparagus, looking for new shoots and eating them raw as they came up. To my young mind, there was something special about this strange plant that could produce six inches of delectable new growth overnight.

Beyond the asparagus field there was a woodlot whose owner lived in town. I think it was more or less abandoned too, since the Douglas-firs were twenty-five feet high and incredibly dense. I would shinny up a tree until it began to bend under my weight. When it had bent down far enough, I could grab an adjacent tree, swing over to it and shinny up until it began to bend too. I would repeat the process as I charted my aerial course across the woodlot. The combined smells of asparagus and Douglas-fir pitch have stayed with me ever since, as I move through the latter stages of personal succession.

Gardens may go on forever, but their owners don't. At some point, this private little plot of mine will pass to another set of private hands, those of a stranger, who may revere my creation, but will more likely either ignore it, or plow it up. I myself will go on to be content with whatever joys can be found in apartment balcony gardens and houseplants. Or I can transfer my gardening allegiances and pleasures to an urban park. This latter prospect intrigues and frightens me at the same time. I have been testing these new waters lately by frequent visits to Stanley Park in Vancouver.

One of the largest city parks in North America, Stanley Park is a kaleidoscope, an encyclopedia of our urban relationship to nature. Deep in its mossy core are stands of rainforest vegetation that verge on the primeval, and on its periphery one finds English rose gardens and children's train rides. Towering cedars abound, but because of heart rot, no one knows for sure how old they are. During the day, a group of volunteers known as the "Ivy League" fan out into the forest to remove invading English ivy. At night, along the same pathways, gay men have their stroll. A frantic, four-lane traffic artery, part of Canada's national highway, bisects the middle of the Park. Individual nature epiphanies occur on the same terrain as drug deals, rapes and occasional murders. Stanley Park embodies all of the magnificence, banality and tragedy of nature within the urban metropolis.

There is water everywhere in Stanley Park, surrounding its peninsula, dripping from the cedars, seeping from the spongy forest floor, and nourishing enormous skunk cabbages. A statue of the Scottish poet Robbie Burns stands on a groomed lawn, and deeper in the forest is a cairn containing the ashes of the First Nation poet Pauline Johnston. There is a community garden, and a cricket pitch. Gaggles of Asian tourists on tight schedules share the walkways with bemused naturalists in Goretex. Stanley Park embodies the contradictions of gardening in close proximity to wild nature. Somehow the Park's elegant, manicured rose garden pales in comparison to the shaggy and towering rainforest just behind it. The gardening impulse is humbled in the face of such magnificence.

In spite of the Park's wild aspects, Vancouverites have an intimate, comfortable connection with it. Naturally, they felt horrified and betrayed when a vicious 2006 windstorm laid waste to large swaths of the Park. What were once majestic cedar and Douglas-fir stands became chaotic jungles of downed trees and branches and uprooted root crowns. The whole city went into shock. This was, after all, *their* park, mandated for Sunday strolls, jogging workouts and wedding photographs. Politicians came, wearing dark suits and looks of grave concern, to stand for photo opportunities next to splintered Douglas-firs. A veritable public witch hunt ensued, but was unable to locate and lay blame at the foot of some corrupt public official or wrongheaded park policy. For many, the Stanley Park windthrow was their first real exposure to the world of natural disturbance events, which alter nature in unpredictable ways, totally without our involvement.

Lord Stanley's Park teems with wildlife, and is a wonderful laboratory for observing how urban folks interact with animals. The Park has provided many a Vancouver child with revelatory first experiences of non-human life. The large and riotous popula-tions of ducks, geese, swans, squirrels and raccoons present a special headache for Parks staff: a strict anti-feeding bylaw is blatantly ignored, particularly by older people. Many seniors maintain daily animal feeding routines. They frequent favoured locations in the Park, and even select individual animals for special treatment. Some carry their bags of grain or nuts in granny carts. A particular animal may get fed by a dozen different people in the course of a day, but for each individual feeding them, the bonding experience is totally unique. Outlandish highrise apartment towers are a stone's throw away and four lanes of traffic pulse madly along nearby Georgia Street, but as the senior citizen and the grey squirrel sit quietly and interact through the medium of unshelled peanuts, the relationship is just as primeval, and intense, as the first encounter between wild human and wild dog.

I fully expect to join this park bench society before long.

Like so many other things we have taken for granted, the suburban lot is coming under scrutiny. Until now, our urban settlement framework has been able to provide us with that two-tenths of a hectare in which to garden, play with the dog, and set our house off in the manorial splendor it deserves. In the end, the traditional suburban lot is probably unsustainable; each new one requires such an increment of habitat, roads, utilities, infrastructure, energy consumption and commuting time that the whole urban organism is stumbling toward collapse. So enhanced streetscaping and public gardens like Stanley Park may in the future become the alternative to the private suburban lot, evolving from delightful frivolity to social necessity.

One wag stated he was "all in favour of urban growth, as long as it doesn't involve density or sprawl." As our city populations grow inexorably, densification is by far the best of two difficult choices. Our domestic landscape architecture needs to rise up and meet the densification challenge. As the amount of green space is slowly whittled down through infill, multifamily, secondary suite and granny flat housing, our landscaping must do more with less. As one descended from the grimy hovel — as opposed to the manorial — tradition, I'd have to say that is a good thing.

Somewhere in all this cornucopia that an urban park offers, I will need to find my niche. I am sure there will be one for me, as the slow whittling down of park maintenance staff continues everywhere, and in quiet desperation, non-profit societies and cadres of volunteers step into the breach. There are rhodos to maintain, ivy to pull, insects to monitor. I could be one of those volunteers, but I would first have to overcome my reluctance to invest time in a public gardening project, which could easily be vandalized. I know how Mahatma Gandhi would address my concern; he would say rebuild the garden, over and over again if necessary. And don't forget to invite the vandals to tea, he would admonish, and be sure they pick the lilacs.

CATEGORIES AND CALYCES

A NATURALIST ONCE wondered out loud why, given the amazing diversity of the earth's creatures, we do not all live in a perpetual state of awe and astonishment. Take British Columbia, for example. A volume on my bookshelf lists the names of all the plants — native, introduced, escaped, subspecies, varieties and hybrids — that are found outside of gardens in this Province. That volume contains 7500 entries. Recently I had occasion to need a list of the Province's vertebrate species, and I was surprised to find 1500 entries. There is no invertebrate list for British Columbia, probably because there aren't enough entomologists to compile it. *Hortus Third*, perhaps the most authoritative listing of all North American ornamental plants, contains 24,000 entries. If I computed all the species within my local reach, both native and introduced, from microbe to moose, sunflower to cedar, speckled dace to alligator lizard, and ladybug to ladyslipper, the number could easily reach a hundred thousand; and that is only counting the ones we know about.

Standing in awe of this diversity, I also sit in admiration of the taxonomists who catalogue it. They respond to some deep-seated need to identify, name and classify. The origin of this urge is frequently traced back to the Swedish botanist Carl Linnaeus, but in truth, if Mr. Linnaeus had never lived, our category-obsessed Western culture would surely have spun off someone else to put forward a system of universal nomenclature. We are that driven.

The Linnaean system of classifying plants is based largely on the nature of reproduction (apparently Mr. Linnaeus had quite a libido) and the structure of flowers. As a result, I am condemned to mediocre taxonomy skills, since I don't really understand flowers. However, I possess a legitimate and signed excuse for this mediocrity. It has to do with my fatal attraction for things that are absurdly and irrationally complex, like grape growing, model airplanes, and the English language. My doctor says I have to avoid prolonged contact with flowers, for fear of falling down the obsessive rabbit hole of calyces, cryptorchs, cymoids, lactifers, drupes and stigmata.

Flowers are for reproduction. Given that there is little emotional baggage attached to plant sex, this should be a straightforward proposition. If you are a flower and you want insects to cross-fertilize you with pollen from other flowers of your same species, it appears to be a fairly simple matter. First you would put out an invitation, in the form of sweet nectar, edible pollen, a nice smell, or maybe just a nice colour. Then you would put your male and female parts right out in the open, about half a bug length apart, so the insects are going to bump into them as they accept your invitation. Many insects are fairly clumsy — witness the barely controlled crash a bumblebee makes every time it lands on a flower — so that shouldn't be too difficult. Then you would make your pollen slightly sticky, so it adheres to the legs, body and underarm hair of your visiting insect. Then you would create a flaring female surface — also sticky — to receive the pollen. You would place that female surface so your clumsy, pollen-encrusted visitor, as it stumbles about knocking over your furniture, will drag its body across it and unwittingly deposit a cargo of pollen. You will set up this arrangement so as to give preference to pollen from another flower rather than from your own, since your species does best with a constant mixing of genetic material. But you might want to incorporate a fail-safe backup to pollinate yourself, if the cross-pollination doesn't happen for some reason. If you want to accessorize, clever little tripping options are available that smack down upon the arriving insect and shower it with pollen. Or you can put your nectar down deep in your floral throat so you can only be pollinated by long-tongued butterflies, a classy option that definitely sets you a cut above your neighbours.

So who would ever expect that the responses to this fairly straightforward pollination proposition are so myriad, so Byzantine, so downright bizarre in their complexity?

On summer weekends, I go to our local farmer's market, which is far more about Third World lifestyle experimentation than it is about farming. Browsing along tables filled with beadwork, tie-dye and pottery, eventually I find one with a few tomatoes and green onions, but not before I have been waylaid by the dreaded book table. Run by a couple of young bibliophiles, this itinerant used bookstore lives in cardboard boxes which are regularly unpacked at farmers markets around the area. I nearly always find some volume on their table that I never knew I needed but now must absolutely have. I frequently accuse this young couple of practicing unethical psychic consumer research on me. One of their recent must-have selections was a delightful little chapbook called *The Secret Life of the Flowers*, written and illustrated by Ann Ophelia Dowden. I was pretty sure I could sample this small book, which looked to be written for young adults, without fear of addiction. So I bought it as a controlled dose, a kind of floristic methadone.

There is a certain traditional snobbery associated with gardens, and I assumed the little chapbook would be the vanity publication of some wealthy socialite who dabbled in painting flowers. Prepared to dislike the book from the start, I quickly realized that Ann Ophelia Dowden was no dabbler, but a real professional who invested great artistic detail in her gorgeously precise watercolours. Not only that, she thoroughly understood the complex pollination mechanisms, which she described in the accompanying text. I went on to discover that Dowden, who at this writing is in her late nineties, is considered the dean of botanical illustration. A professional artist by trade and naturalist by inclination, she turned to flowers early in her career and never looked back, writing and illustrating ten flower books on her own, and illustrating eight others.

Reading on, I felt myself flirting once more with the yawning rabbit hole of floral addiction. Of course Dowden would have to include a chapter on the yucca, that spiky desert ornamental that takes reproductive irrationality to dizzyingly addictive proportions.

The yucca is a large New World genus native to the American southwest and Mexico. Species can range from teacup to tree size, but all are characterized by spiky leaves and large, showy flowers. A number have made their way into the horticultural trade, and can be successfully grown in some surprisingly non-desert climates. The yucca has a single, "obligate" pollinator, a little white moth called — aptly — the yucca moth. When the yucca flower is ready for pollination, the yucca moth arrives and goes from plant to plant, collecting a ball of pollen. When the pollen ball is large enough, the moth selects a certain yucca flower to actually pollinate. But first she unsheathes a sharp ovipositor, penetrates the selected flower's ovary walls, and inserts her eggs. When that is finished, she goes to the top of the flower, and carefully stuffs her ball of male pollen down into the yucca flower's vase-shaped pollen receptacle, the stigma. She then flies off, repeats this process several times, and dies, never having visited any other flower but the yucca, and never having eaten anything — no nectar, no pollen, nothing. The doubly impregnated yucca flower then grows into a large, tough ovary structure full of developing yucca seeds and moth larvae. The moth larvae eat some of the seeds as they develop, but they never eat them all. When the larvae have reached maturity, they tunnel out through the mature seed capsule and drop to the ground, whereupon they gestate into moth-hood, and carry on the life cycle.

This arrangement makes absolutely no sense. Why would the yucca tie its fortunes to a single moth? Why would the moth do the same? What if it is a good year for moths and a bad year for yuccas? How did this bizarre relationship develop? An arrangement that complex could not just occur spontaneously, but if it didn't, what were the early stages of this relationship (drinks and a movie?) that encouraged the two species to go ahead and form a permanent and perilous union?

The yucca moth can't cheat: if she lays her eggs in a flower but doesn't pollinate it, her eggs don't develop. How does she know that? And what prevents her from inserting a whole bunch of eggs into a flower to maximize her offspring, who then go on to lay waste to *all* the seeds in that capsule? What is the nature of the information flow that provides the positive and negative feedback as plant and moth steer this incredibly risky evolutionary course? Now there are a few questions for my garden bench.

A tiny population of native yucca (*Yucca glauca*) exists in Canada, along the Alberta-Montana border. Some people will go fifteen hundred kilometres to see Disneyland, but I drove that distance to see the Canadian yucca population, which occupies a remote area about the size of two football fields. It was an ecological pilgrimage, to pay homage to one of nature's more desperate arrangements. The yucca plant is esthetically suited to the tortuous badland country it grows in — a basal fan of tough, spiky leaves, with a tall and woody floral stalk emerging from the middle of the fan. For a precious few days in summer, the stalk is festooned with delicate, luminous flowers the colour of thick cream. It is like the plant has absorbed all the harshness of its landscape to produce a brief moment of lushness.

It is one thing to be a yucca in New Mexico, surrounded by your comrades and comfortable knowing you are at the centre of origin of your genus and all its complex reproductive baggage. But think of being a yucca in Alberta's badlands: you are literally, and figuratively, at the end of the road. You have no comrades to the north of you, or to the east or west, for that matter. Life is tough here, and the prevailing climate is sending you a strong message that you're lucky to be here at all. You would think, under these incredibly marginal badlands circumstances, yucca would drop the crazy moth arrangement and go with something more conventional; there is too much that can go wrong. But no.

My Alberta yucca pilgrimage was too late in the season for me to witness pollination, but I could see the telltale little holes drilled into the side of each egg-shaped seedpod by the escaping larvae. The Quixotic yucca pollination arrangement still holds, even in the harshness of the Alberta badlands. I sense echoes of that same stubborn adherence to complexity and irrationality in my own garden.

Plant taxonomists talk glibly about "primitive" flowers and "advanced" flowers. The primitive flowers, they argue, have simple and symmetrical reproductive structures, which are placed right out in the open. Advanced flowers are asymmetrical, with many unique parts. I confess to some nagging doubts about this theory (the yucca flower is symmetrical, for instance). We can logically assume that complex and specialized floral structures evolved from simpler ones, but I'm not that certain that all simple structures are "primitive". The dandelion flower is considered primitive, since it has many simple parts rather than few specialized ones, and it is radially symmetrical. But the arrangement has worked splendidly, exuberantly well. The dandelion flower is not primitive, it is rather a perfect, economical marriage of form and function.

I wonder what it would be like to organize a garden along Linnaean taxonomic lines, starting with mosses and lichens, then moving on to another part of the yard to the ferns, and then to the conifers. Arriving at the angiosperms (basically everything besides mosses, lichens, ferns and conifers), one would organize the garden layout based on the taxonomic principle of simplicity versus specialization. Such a garden would help me learn taxonomy, but I shouldn't think it would be very interesting. I rather like the idea of growing yuccas together with dandelions.

HERE IF ANYWHERE

MY MOTHER LOVED plants. Both her parents died when I was little, but I got a sense of my mother's upbringing through family visits with her three aunts. Emma, Lena and Annie were all tall, rawboned Norwegian women whose lives — at least to my young eyes — seemed to revolve around flowers, fresh rhubarb, and Gravenstein apples. My mother carried that family penchant forward, and gardened all her life. She was also an adept bridge player, and the first signs of Alzheimer's curse came when the game began to confuse her. By the time she was in her early seventies, my mother's world became progressively smaller, and more temporary. But she continued to garden. The neural connections she needed to plant, prune and water remained firmly in place. My father made sure that potting soil, trowels and inexpensive annuals were always on hand for her to work with. She would re-pot the same plants several times a week, taking obvious satisfaction and even joy in working with the black, pungent soil, the tactile roughness of unglazed ceramic pots, and the delicate magic of leaves, stems and roots. Even when she moved from home into an Alzheimer's ward, the potting and re-potting continued. Gardening was one of her last abilities to go.

I have no way of knowing for sure whether plants and soil made my mother's later life less anxious. It seemed so, but perhaps her gardening simply put the rest of the family more at ease. Like the gift, the garden is reciprocal; it bestows on both receiver and giver. This reciprocity may be a primary mechanism of the emerging discipline of horticultural or garden therapy — the provision of gardens for those who are troubled, infirm, convalescing or dying. Providing a therapy garden for others is not only a benevolent and reciprocal gesture, it may also be a subtle way of affirming the garden's importance to our own lives.

Knowledge of the curative powers of gardens and nature goes back to antiquity, but to modern medicine it came as a revelation, when by sheer accident some wealthy patron donated funds for a hospital garden, and staff began reporting on anomalous health improvements in patients who made use of it. Academia quickly appropriated the idea. Borrowing heavily from the field of environmental and eco-psychology, the academic psychologists began churning out grant proposals, theses, scholarly publications and even some original research. Their findings identified patient stress release as one of the key therapeutic mechanisms of horticultural or garden therapy. They conducted a suite of experiments where subjects were placed in mildly stressful situations, and then recovery time from that stress was measured as the subject views scenes of natural environments, totally built environments, and built environments with trees and shrubs added in. Predictably, the indicators of stress levels dropped most quickly in the group exposed to natural environment scenes and slowest in those viewing totally built environments.

To date, horticultural therapy has focussed mainly on providing gardens and indoor plants in hospitals and other health facilities. Interestingly, the therapeutic benefits seem to arise from the patient's sense of autonomy. Stressed patients are unhealthy patients, requiring longer hospital stays and more medication. Much of the stress hospital and other health facility patients experience originates from the lack of control they have over their own daily lives and routines. The provision of a garden is one way of giving back a tiny bit; patients make their own decision to go into the familiar environment of the garden, and while there, they are not surrounded by medical staff, instruments and sterile walls. They can decide to stand or sit, smell a rose or not, move to the sunny side or stay in the shade. The hospital garden visitor gives himself or herself permission to take a brief mental holiday from the world of medicine and illness.

Some researchers see the mechanisms of garden therapy from an anthropological perspective: when our senses tell us we have come into a lush, productive environment that will quench our thirst, feed us and shelter us, an ancient gene switches on, telling us to relax, let down defenses, and recover from the rigours of daily survival.

Steven Kaplan, one of the pioneers in the field of environmental psychology, sees two different modes of consciousness. One he refers to as "directed attention" — voluntary and prolonged attention, which demands effort and makes us subject to fatigue. Directed attention is a curious phenomenon, one that permits us to become scholars, artists, musicians, and so on. It is the diametric opposite of the second mode, "general awareness," a kind of roving and relaxed attention to surroundings that we employ when we are outside, in nature. Both forms of consciousness are vital to the modern human, so Kaplan proposes that we alleviate the fatigue generated by directed attention by frequently exercising its less stressful opposite — general awareness. And the logical place to exercise general awareness is in its native setting, nature. Or in its domestic cousin, the garden.

Much of our indoor, directed work engages only one or two senses at a time. But when I am in the garden, a bouquet of sensory impressions arrive simultaneously. On hands and knees grubbing out the inevitable weeds hiding underneath the garden plants, I feel the cool complex of soil under my hand. A cabbage looper flits about on the periphery of my vision. There is the energetic buzz of a massive bumblebee as it works amongst the lavender. As I reach to weed under the salvia, bruised leaves give off the strong scent of culinary sage. A breeze works through the lilac hedge, and lifts the hairs on my bare forearms. From somewhere behind me comes the muffled scratching and snuffling of Spud the dog. I hear the excited lilt of children playing across the street. Hurrah for general awareness; it is far more than just a brief respite from directed attention. Perhaps the successful alternation of those two states somehow defines the human challenge and the human genius.

My mother's later life became a haunted and desperate quest to connect to events, faces and memories. Food was a problem. She could finish a meal and minutes later, have no recollection of it. And yet there were two activities that she not only remembered to do, but how to do: feeding birds, and gardening. The sequence of actions required to plant a geranium or water a flowerbed, somehow remained crystal clear.

So there are many explanations for the therapeutic value of gardens, including one based on simplicity; that a garden is inherently simpler, and thus more understandable, than a built environment. I totally reject that one. I see a typical large urban centre dominated by highrise buildings, automobiles and street signs as criminally simple, and the garden as a wellspring of unfolding complexity. My guess is the mechanisms of garden therapy are ultimately unknowable, as are the basic transactions between people and nature.

My own therapeutic uses of the garden are not overt, probably due to an upbringing that places me squarely in the old-school tradition of the rigid male who avoids the issue of feelings. It is far easier for me to envision horticultural therapy for others than for myself. However I can easily acknowledge the personal value of my garden for *recreational* therapy, which perhaps crosses over.

I have occasional days at work that are inconclusive and unsatisfying; this seems to go with the working territory. Coming home from one of those frustrating days to the garden can be great refreshment. Even in the most evolved and multifaceted garden, there is ongoing, tangible work to be done. And the nature of that work is refreshingly straightforward. If you have weeds, you weed. If a hedge has gone out of control, you trim it. I like that simplicity, and sometimes I absolutely revel in it.

I don't really like the term garden therapy. It implies a kind of selfish, one-way approach: a quick visit to the wisterias and the peonies, and then you're good for another three weeks. I believe the true therapeutic aspects are found in ongoing garden transactions, from esthetics, to planning, to weeding. Gardening and landscaping are also useful forms of temporary withdrawal from the onrush of daily demands.

My transactional garden therapy is combined with pet therapy, since whenever I am in the yard, a furry brown presence is there too, snuffling about or waiting for me to dig dandelions.

At age eleven, our daughter Amy was having a summer of discovery, learning about the joys of softball, horseback riding, and boys. A healthy and vibrant child, she was suddenly ripped from our lives by an undiagnosed congenital brain aneurysm. In the chaotic days that followed this shattering event, we realized the need for some kind of memorial service. Something, some event to let Amy's friends and their parents honour her life, and to provide a kind of symbolic closure for us, even though the pain of losing her continues to this day. As we thought about this memorial, no indoor location seemed suitable, but then we found that a small island could be rented for events. Situated in a lake in Regina's Wascana Park, it was accessible by a tiny passenger ferry. The centre of the oval-shaped island was grassy, and the shoreline was ringed by mature weeping willows. Like Monet's watergarden, some effort had been expended to make this islet look natural. People came to the memorial on the islet — families, teachers, neighbours, members of Amy's softball team. We spoke, we were silent, we cried, we walked in contemplation, and we even managed to laugh, remembering some of her silly childhood antics. The island's space provided room for adults to gather or be alone, for children to play on the grass, and for a table with pictures of Amy. We brought a tape player so we could play her favourite music, the theme from *Chariots of Fire*. If there was a need for some over arching presence, it was provided by the timeless weeping willows.

I am forever grateful to that islet, and its willows. Perhaps this was prefigured by a passage in Kenneth Grahame's classic children's book, *The Wind in the Willows*. In a chapter entitled "The Piper at the Gates of Dawn", which I first read at about Amy's age, I remember being moved closer to religious feeling than anything else I have experienced since. In the chapter, the two characters Mole and his friend Rat go off downriver in search of a baby otter, who is lost and feared dead. After a futile, all-night search, they come to a small island, just at daybreak:

> Slowly, but with no doubt or hesitation whatsoever, and in something of a solemn expectancy, the two animals passed through the broken, tumultuous water and moored their boat at the flowery margin of the island. In silence they landed, and pushed through the blossom and scented herbage and undergrowth that led up to the level ground, until they stood on a little lawn of a marvellous green, set round with Nature's own orchard trees — crab-apple, wild cherry, and sloe. "This is the place of my song-dream, the place the music played to me," said Rat, as if in a trance. "Here, in this holy place, here if anywhere, surely we shall find Him!"

The Him Rat refers to is Pan, the bearded demigod of nature, half-man, half goat. Pan has rescued Portly, the baby otter, and returns him to the grateful Mole and Rat. Then Pan bestows on all of them the gift of forgetfulness, "lest the awful remembrance should remain and grow, and overshadow mirth and pleasure, and the great haunting memory should spoil all the after-lives of animals helped out of difficulties."

When I am on long road trips I like to break them up with short explorations, of hillsides I've never walked before, coffee shops I've never been in, and so on. Another diversion is to collect archival photographs of landscapes from museums and archives along my routes, and then try to relocate and rephotograph them. Repetitive drives are where I need these activities the most, to break the monotony, get out of my head, and reconnect to the landscape. During one such trip eastward through the Purcell Mountains, I stopped at a small-town nursery, to stretch my legs and look around for a bit.

When I finished touring the greenhouse, I backed out of the crowded parking lot and drove down a narrow farm lane between two orchards, looking for a convenient place to turn around and get back on the highway. I did find a turnaround, but just beyond it, I discovered a spectacular, neglected garden. The nursery owners were in full spring frenzy, so I decided to ask permission after the fact, and slipped into the unknown garden, with camera and notebook. The flower beds had gone to weeds and the rank grass was uncut, but the original gardener, whoever it was, obviously had a keen eye for trees. Besides the usual maples and elms, there were oaks, hickories, catalpas and other eastern hardwood species I barely recognized. Evergreens were also present, but in small numbers. The whole town was surrounded by landscapes of Douglas-fir forest, which are awfully hard to improve upon, and this gardener was smart enough not to try. Walking further, I realized that I was in quite a large private garden, spread over a couple of acres of rolling terrain. The adjacent properties were all orchards, and from within the garden, the hum of town and highway were barely audible. A small creek crossed diagonally through the garden, and refreshingly, it had not been shackled into a narrow channel and so was full of riotous cattails. In contrast to the typical garden, where one's focus is directed toward the ground, here I was looking up and out, into mature tree canopies, tree groupings, and layered tree backgrounds. Obviously no one had touched the trees in years, but they had been well pruned early on, so even in neglect, they maintained graceful and sustainable shapes.

Reaching the far corner of the property, I entered into a formal rose garden, also abandoned, that was enclosed by a high cedar hedge. The placement of this garden was interesting, since it could only be accessed by traversing the entire length of the property first. By this time my day's trip schedule was getting way out of whack, but my curiosity about this garden was whetted, and I felt compelled to visit every corner, writing notes and taking photographs. I catalogued what this anonymous master gardener had created: an open, grassy entrance, inviting the visitor to probe leafier garden depths. To one side of the entrance, a small gazebo, badly weathered, inviting a sit before or after the garden walk. Next, a sloping dell leading down to creek, weeping willow, cattails and a tiny arched footbridge. Then a climb back up again, following a winding path to a rocky knob planted to shrubs and conifers. Then back off the knob to a classic English park (or African savanna) of level grass and scattered, high-canopy oaks and other broadleaved trees. A water feature, in the form of a concrete fishpond (now empty and badly cracked). And finally, to the private sanctum of the rose garden.

Fancying myself the forensic anthropologist piecing together a lost culture through observation and deduction, I began to build up a profile of this mystery gardener. I wrote: "the individual would likely have been a man, based on the amount of sheer bullwork involved in moving that much soil, trees and concrete. Probably an older one, with some degree of financial success to allow for his indulgence. And perhaps a fairly private individual, who could nurture and sustain this amazing garden blueprint over the years it took to complete it. Subject was able to, either through direct experience or study, learn the needs and adaptations of the eastern hardwoods. Subject had the ability to create half a dozen separate environments and mesh them into a harmonious whole."

Some weeks later I travelled that route again and stopped at the nursery, to ask belated permission from the owners and find out more about the garden. They confirmed the garden builder was a successful orchardist, who had passed away a few years previously, and that he had built it as memorial garden when his beloved wife died. The new owners were concerned about the state of the garden, but were completely absorbed in starting their nursery enterprise, and had no spare time to work on it. I asked and was granted permission to come back occasionally, to see the garden in different seasons and perhaps better understand its logic.

A garden in memoriam to a dead spouse or family member presents a conundrum. When the builder — the memorialist — passes on, the garden faces abandonment, since no one else is likely to carry the same level of devotion. The death of a memorial garden becomes a subsequent tragedy. So I concluded that a grieving spouse or relative must turn the memorial urge into a more communal, enduring statement, making the garden a celebration of marital or filial love, an ode to the small joys of living, or simply a poem to the delights of the garden — this verdant clasp of hands between nature and ourselves.

But still, there was something fascinating about this abandoned garden which drew me back. Seeing which cultivated species persisted and which native species crept back in was interesting enough, but the real fascination was in the abandonment itself. Part of the attraction is the vaguely morbid spectacle of watching plans and dreams brought inevitably to ruin. But there is another part of the fascination which is more forensic. The asking of "what was intended here?", "what went wrong?" and "are my works following the same ill-fated pattern?" This explains some of the enduring popularity of J.E.H. MacDonald's famous painting, *The Tangled Garden*. MacDonald, a stalwart of the Canadian Group of Seven painters, captured the essence of the wilding process in his painting, portraying feral hollyhocks and rogue sunflowers in an abandoned garden setting. Some garden designers deliberately set out for this look, creating what is known as the "ruins garden". The over-arching symbol of the ruins garden, our visual clue to the landscape's meaning, is the partly toppled Ionic column, with ivy growing over it. An iconic remnant of a once mighty human enterprise. Gazing upon the abandoned foundations, toppled columns and broken statuary of the ruins garden encourages us to speculate on human vanity, on the impermanence of civilizations, and on nature's boundless ability to resurrect itself.

GARDENING DRY

WORKING IN A dry climate fundamentally changed my notions of the garden. The ground for this voyage of discovery was a large urban yard in the South Okanagan. The original homeowner had traditional suburban landscaping ambitions, which eventually ran aground for lack of water. The next occupants were a series of renters, who ignored the yard. A woefully inappropriate blue spruce in the front yard had somehow made it to pole size, after which its dead skeleton gradually bleached white in the fierce summer sun. The only real survivors were a forsythia and a dusty, sprawling juniper. The front lawn was parched and dusty, with cheatgrass in the high spots and quackgrass in the low. The few remaining lawn fescues had long since reverted to their feral bunchgrass growth form. The only thing separating the front yard from a look of complete abandonment was the absence of a junker car on blocks and a dead washing machine.

This yard was not only in a dry climate, it was growing on a very rapidly-draining soil. A rough gauge of a soil's water holding capacity is to dig a small hole, fill it with water, and see how long it takes to drain. A few minutes is typical for very coarse soils, an hour or more for heavy clay soils. My test hole drained as I filled it. But the local climate bore wonderful gardening potential; nearly 150 frost-free days, fairly benign winters, and none of the slugs, wilts and molds of wetter environments.

I decided on a total renovation. The old lawn, as well as the cratered driveway that ran through the middle of it, had to go. When I made that decision, I knew that the soil needed a boost of organic matter to retain more water, but was still blissfully unaware of the extent of riverstone that it hid below the surface. The local landfill was making compost from ground wood waste and biosolids, so I hauled in and spread several loads of the stuff on the old lawn. Then early one Saturday morning I went to the local rental shop and secured a brand spanking new eight horsepower, self-propelled, three-speed rototiller for the day. Donning sturdy boots and work gloves, I was going to employ agronomic skill plus eight horses of brute force to manhandle the old lawn into a deeply composted, fine seedbed. The rototiller had a single shank in back of the curved blades, which the lady at the rental shop explained you could use kind of like a pivot point. By pushing down on the handles, the shank would dig in and hold the rototiller back while the rotating blades dug deeply into the soil. I started the machine, walked it to the corner of the yard, grasped the handles firmly, and engaged first gear. For a few precious seconds, the blades churned, and dirt and cheatgrass began to fly. Then came a horrendous clanging sound — like hitting a bell with a sledge-hammer — and the machine bucked, lifted right up out of the ground, and proceeded to trundle off down the lawn without me. I rescued the machine, steered it back to the start point, and tried again, knowing each powered implement has its own learning curve. I had probably just caught some isolated rock at a bad angle, which bumped the tiller up and out of the soil.

I soon discovered that no matter how much finesse I applied to the rototiller, it bucked up immediately. I stopped it and got out a shovel to investigate, and realized that the rototiller blades were being rejected by a luxurious and firmly embedded carpet of riverstone lying a knuckle joint or two below the surface. I tried the shovel in several other parts of the yard and had a stunning moment of geological insight. I was living on a glacio-fluvial terrace.

To get my money's worth, I played with the rototiller the rest of the day, putting the relatively stoneless top three centimeters of soil into a fine tilth. And then I closed the rototiller chapter and got out the shovel again. It is remarkable how chance and events conspire to lead me away from using gasoline in the garden.

The shovel work started slowly. A firm, foot-assisted plunge rarely got the blade down more than a few centimeters before it clanged to a full stop against a stone. Mostly rounded granite, these subterranean offenders ranged through plum (I ignored anything smaller), peach, potato, and canteloupe size, all the way up to watermelons, with the median range somewhere between potato and cantaloupe. Together, they constituted an absolute celebration, a lithic orgasm. Digging was intensely frustrating. When I hit a rock, I had to scrabble around it to find the perimeter, plunge the shovel deep enough to hook an edge, and then gently lever it out, mindful of my twice-split, twice-repaired shovel handle. To get one rock out, I typically had to first loosen the five adjacent rocks that held it tightly in place.

Occasionally I had to use a prybar to loosen the larger rocks. One of the shovel entertainments I indulged in was to imagine the rush of those periglacial rivers as they bounced these rocks around, ground them down, and packed them tightly into my yard. The bench that I lived on was nearly 300 meters above the bottom of the Okanagan valley, but at one point the glacier that filled the valley was at the same level as my house, and a riotous meltwater river flowed along the *top* of the glacier, spreading its generous bedload of stone and creating my level bench. Like certain other types of manual labour, shoveling gives you the time — and the rhythm — to think. And I think a lot about how I was victimized by a glacier.

There are two upsides to landscaping on a glaciofluvial terrace. The stones are all small enough to be moved by hand. I'm not sure why that is; maybe the big leviathans are actually there, but lurking below my two-shovel maximum working depth. The second benefit is the abundance of material for stonework projects. But with rounded glaciofluvial rocks, drypointing is not an option: any wall or structure made with riverstone demands cement.

As I dug up the yard, I settled into a routine of creating an angled face between the dug and undug. Face the dug portion, and work backward into new ground. This provided the tough mass of soil and stone under the shovel blade with a collapse route, into the dug portion. A firm shovel plant, followed by the first foot shiver against the shovel step. If the soil mass doesn't give way, then decrease the shovel angle to the ground, and give another foot thrust. Eventually the soil and stones release, and slip toward the dug side. Then pick the watermelon and cantaloupe rocks out of the dug side by hand, and switch to the rake to get the rest.

A rigid, steel-tined rake is almost a forgotten object in the gardening tool shed, but it is a backbreakingly precise tool for preparing raw land. Beyond its default talents for gathering up leaves and levelling soil, it is a great collector and sorter of rocks. By gradually raking the rocks over to a raised edge, you can raise the loaded rake slightly, shake the soil out, and then beach the rocks to be later collected and removed. The rocks that fall through the tines are small enough not to bruise a bare foot or tangle with a lawn mower blade.

I worked on cattle ranches in my younger days, and did lots of shovel work, digging postholes and clearing trash from irrigation ditches. One boss, a particularly hard-bitten rancher, had a venerable shovel with an absolutely smooth, honey-coloured handle and a blade whose point was completely worn away. Instead of looking like the bottom of a heart shape, this shovel blade looked more like the top, with two lobes and a depression in the middle, where the original point used to be. The handle was strong, the blade sharp, but the shovel's face had been completely customized by long contact with gravel and stone. I remember speculating at the time how much digging, how many stones it must have taken for the rancher to completely wear away two inches of metal. Now I know.

I am tempted to think that stones go with dry climates, and they do, to some extent. The bottoms and sides of river valleys — which is where river stones get deposited, tend toward a dry climate. And glacial moraines, which are full of stones, can be droughty. And then there is glacial till, full of sharp rather than water-rounded rocks, which is found extensively in prairie climates. The answer, truly, is that stones are everywhere, kind of like mosquitoes.

I have always had a certain need and affinity for manual labour. I like engaging those big, slow-twitch muscles of arm and back and leg, I like the sense of tangible progress in building a fence or digging a trench or splitting a cord of firewood. I like the humble tools and I like the feel of leather gloves once the work has molded them to my hands. My first summer job, when I was twelve and no one had ever heard of big round bales, was putting up hay. I delighted in swinging the rectangular bales of alfalfa and timothy up onto a hay wagon, and unloading them into the barn. One old fellow I worked for had us stack the hay in the second story of his big barn. The hay storage area had a smooth wood floor. You could stand at the front end of the barn and if you threw the bale hard enough, usually with a kind of discus windup and release, you could slide it on the polished wood surface all the way to the back end of the barn.

Physical labour has always come easy for me, but not without a sense of ambivalence. Putting up hay, digging postholes, splitting firewood, sledgehammering rocks, operating a wheelbarrow, and shovelling has the stigma of downscale, minimum-wage, job-ghetto work, to be studiously avoided. Indeed, the delightful and labour-intensive square bale has been mostly overtaken by the totally tractor-dependent big round bale.

As I got old enough to take summer jobs, my mother was happy to see me working, but she would voice discreet concern about how manual work was not getting me ready for college. My father would say nothing in these discussions. He was a civil engineer, but felt the same guilty pleasure in physical work as I.

My manual yard-shovelling task included getting rid of an old driveway, which ran right through the middle of the yard instead of along the fence line, where it rightly belonged. I have never been able to visualize driveways and automobiles as items of status or esthetics, and I do my best to hide rather than display them. The driveway digging included the usual stones, plus an additional layer of compacted gravel on top. For good measure, broken up bits of an old asphalt surface had to be collected and removed. This was a task with a high humility quotient.

For the next step in renovating the yard, I reached back to the venerable tradition of green manuring — planting a crop and then turning it under to enhance the soil. Originally an agricultural practice, it is now rarely used on a farm scale since it idles a field for an entire growing season. But it is a perfect adjunct to a more patient approach to gardening and landscaping, and can be thought of as composting on a large scale. For my green manure crop, I chose red clover, a favourite of mine. It is aggressively well-behaved, the seeds are large, and they are delightfully cheap. I looked high and low for the specific bacterial inoculant for clover, but none of the farm supply stores carried it, and I was forced to rely on the homegrown bacterial troops in the soil. The ground was still a bit rough, so I bumped up the recommended seeding rate, spread and raked a bit of soil on top, and then relied on a good hour of random criss-cross walking in my Size 15s to pack the seedbed. The seeding caught beautifully, and by late summer the clover was tall enough for the housecat to play stealthy jungle tiger in. I pulled up a few plants to inspect the roots, which were gloriously abundant. Tiny, cream-coloured bumps on the roots reassured me that I was getting adequate nitrogen fixation. There were a few bare spots where the seed didn't catch, so I went back over those, added a bit more compost, and fill-seeded them until I had a continuous sward. Green manures are normally planted in the fall and worked into the soil the next spring, or, like mine, planted in spring for incorporation in the fall, before freeze-up. That fall I got busy with other things, so I let the yard go through the winter, planning to work it in the next spring. When spring came, the clover came up green and vigorous. I fill-seeded a couple of winterkilled patches, and let it grow on into its second summer. The neighbours were curious about this dramatic departure from suburban practice, and often stopped to marvel at the lush greenness of the clover. They also noted the everpresent quackgrass, cheatgrass, dandelions and round-leaved mallow had a difficult time competing with my trifoliate friends.

When legumes bloom, the nitrogen fixation generally shuts right down, so whenever the clover showed flower buds, I got out a manual grass whip and nipped them off. There was no rest for my hardworking bacteria.

One of the nice features of true clovers is that the plants do not become coarse and woody as they mature, like their legume cousins alfalfa and sweetclover do. Red and white clovers are all leaf, petiole and root. When I finally turned the clover crop into the soil, the great mass of roots and greenery broke down right away, moving my semidesert glaciofluvial terrace soil forward toward a rich grassland soil.

Half of xeriscaping, the bottom half, is putting organic matter into the soil so it can capture and hold the reduced amounts of water that you do apply. Most of the watering that I saw my Okanagan neighbours do was simply replenishing some Chthonian underground aquifer, there being nothing to slow the water down beyond the two-inch-deep mat of Kentucky bluegrass roots.

The top half of this new movement is equally fascinating. Xeriscaping is a slow, incremental revolution creeping across the yards of North America, which always scores major victories whenever a local jurisdiction starts charging consumption fees for domestic water use. As citizens, we all have a right to water pure enough to drink, but we don't have the right to slather this carefully treated water indiscriminately onto our lawns. Xeriscaping touches on this profound conundrum of contemporary urban life.

In selecting plants for xeriscaping, drought tolerance is the key factor. The mechanisms of plant drought tolerance are many, but most of them flout our traditional landscaping canon: slow growth, reduced leaf area, summer dormancy, hairy or light-coloured leaves, small flowers, compact stature, and widely-spaced plants.

A great deal of suburban landscaping is token. Drive through any single-family neighbourhood and you will see half a dozen overused and underpruned perennials, providing a complement to the front lawn. They will vary by region, but lean heavily toward cotoneaster, juniper, viburnum, lilacs, maples and so on. They form a kind of check-off, showing that the yard has "been landscaped," and perhaps the plantings will mark out a property line or a driveway. The same approach is used in the cement planters of large parking lots, where asphalt substitutes for grass. Some, like myself, do not find this approach attractive, but it is a readily identifiable and acceptable landscaping template, with a lengthy tradition behind it.

If the same approach of the token checkoff specimen planting is used in xeriscaping, the result will be an aesthetic and ecological disaster, since xeriscaping plants tend to be shorter, less colourful, and more transparent. I often hear xeriscaping mispronounced as "zeroscaping," implying that you have to settle for a landscaping that is practically non-existent. The biggest difficulty in xeriscaping is overcoming the legacy of the lush English garden as our esthetic benchmark for all landscaping.

The true template for the xeriscaper is nature, in the form of dry ecosystems.

Grasslands, deserts, alpine areas and even sand dune vegetation offer natural groupings from which to draw garden inspiration. When I planted a young ponderosa pine — one of our most drought tolerant trees — I wanted it to be part of a group planting, but was unsure of what to put around it. So I tried a couple of different herbaceous plants, just to see how they might look as part of a pine grouping. Bluebunch wheatgrass — another drought-tolerant native — turned out to be the obvious choice. Its tall, narrow leaves and ascending stems nicely complemented the pine's fine sprays of needles. The grouping made ecological as well as esthetic sense, since ponderosa and bluebunch are common companions in the wild.

Another dry template that is permanently etched in my mind is Mitlenatch, a small, rocky and uninhabited islet near Campbell River. In spite of the wet coastal climate that surrounds it, the islet's unique topographical position provides it with a microclimate dry enough for cactus. Stepping ashore, I was confronted with drifts of pink sea blush, interspersed with yellow monkey flower and blue camas, strewn artistically across the rocky slopes. Tiger lily, alumroot, saxifrage, saskatoon and Pacific sanicle were all in flower. This was classic vernal pool ecology; rainfall and nutrients run off the steeper rock faces and accumulate in small basins. So the massive, inhospitable rock surface is punctuated by small riots of floral diversity. The lush interweavings of colour on Mitlenatch were like French Impressionist paintings, but if Claude Monet had seen Mitlenatch, I believe he would have laid his brushes down out of sheer respect.

Trees can play a major role in xeriscaping if chosen, planted and maintained properly. The Okanagan yard had two mature maples in it, which had never been pruned. Garish long sucker branches were everywhere, multiple main branches started from the same point, and the lowest branches started at below head level. I pruned them in stages, and over a three-year period I cut out the suckers and bad forks, and gradually "lifted the crown," so the first branches were just above my reach. This made a huge difference. Mature trees that are pruned to a high but more or less continuous canopy can create a wonderful, low-stress environment underneath. The shade that a mature tree provides will more than offset the water it uses, and the lifted crown allows morning and evening sun to reach the plants underneath, while shielding them from the drying midday sun.

Those Okanagan summers consisted of digging riverstone, hauling countless loads of compost in a ratty trailer that had started life as the back of a half-ton pickup, and watering red clover. But it paid off. Once I worked the clover in, I seeded a tough mixture of sheep fescue and white Dutch clover, and left plenty of bare openings in which to plant drought tolerant native shrubs, forbs and grasses. And I have a massive pyramid of riverstone in one corner of the yard. I think I'll leave it, so that future generations can ponder its meaning.

A Place to Work Things Out

WOOD LILIES (*Lilium philadelphicum*) grow well here. Starting from an initial planting, the lilies have taken over a couple of pockets around the yard. I am not sure how they did this, whether by seed or bulblet, but I welcome their tall, dressy stems and late flowers — the colour of orange peels and rust. The lilies certainly do multiply, and they self-thin as the earliest and biggest stems shade out and suppress the later ones. I like to help out with this thinning process, reaching down through the foliage to grub out the weaker, shorter stems, and making Thoreau's invidious distinctions about morning glories and prickly lettuce at the same time. I know my thinning isn't necessary; the lilies would arrive at an optimum density completely on their own, and the few pallid weeds underneath would never do more than eke out a marginal existence, if I left them. My intervention probably accelerates the thinning process by a few days, and the final plant density is going to be a bit less than what the lilies would achieve on their own. But the great benefit is that I get to participate. The wood lilies seem to invite me to do this, although cautiously, since their stems and leaves are surprisingly brittle. I do contribute my bit of ecological randomness when I leave a parsley that has crept in amongst the lilies, just for the pleasing conjunction of deep green leaves against those of an even deeper green.

Thinning and its sister activity, pruning, are profound and passionate activities for me. They bring me into intimate contact with plant personalities. I am particularly fascinated by the pruning and training of grapes. I started that learning curve after the bleeding Concord incident, but could not leave it alone once I discovered there were five major grape pruning systems and dozens of variants. The complex series of sequenced grapevine growth events is slowly becoming clear to me, as well as the ways and means of intervening sympathetically in that sequence. As I sit in under my little arbour, I am beginning to see various aspects of the grape plant's form and function. A bonus is that I have learned what I know of viticulture from interesting men and women. These people have convinced me that we probably know the grape plant more intimately than any other species, with the possible exception of corn, and we are more hands-on with grapes than with any other species. To grow grapes is to handle vines — pruning, suckering, thinning, training, harvesting. Grapes are perhaps the last great holdout in our desperate drive to mechanize every aspect of agriculture and horticulture.

The roots of grapes explore deep into the soil strata. Wines from old vineyards are often prized, since they access particular combinations of deep minerals that younger vines cannot. Grapes also root into cultural strata; different varieties and pruning systems and vinting processes reflect the various regions of Europe where they originated. It is not surprising that our increasingly automated and rootless society is joyously embracing wine, a stubbornly local and largely handmade product. The *terroir* of a region is the combination of local climatic, geological and cultural factors that make its wines different from those of another region. *Terroir* is, in effect, a message in a bottle. That message is a local connection with the earth, and local human adaptation to the earth.

When I thin, or prune, I am a junior apprentice to a master natural process, and I sense the master wants me to learn. It could be saying, perhaps in the deep and compelling voice of Pan, *"here is a growth system where I flower on one-year-old wood, and if you, shallow apprentice, think about this growth system, it will become clear to you that I must be pruned differently than plants that flower on current-year wood. As I manifest myself in the constant lilac, I secure my continued presence by both my suckers and my flowers, but I will work with you if you wish to shift my balance some way toward flowering. And I will welcome you into the world of my wood lilies, so long as you understand and respect their needs. I will present you with multiple confusions of taxonomy and weather, but will also remind you that these are not at all confusing to me. If you let me, I will involve you in the lives of organisms not alien, but completely different from you. Different in size, life cycle, timescale, physiology, reproduction. And as you grow in understanding of those biological patterns and of those different lives, perhaps your own life will find its quiet order."*

When there are personal and perhaps Difficult Things to Work Out, people gravitate to favoured places. Some prefer pubs, others opt for libraries, park benches, or mountaintops. My place is in the garden. The rumination engine can run on as I weed, or cultivate, lie in the hammock, or sit under the grape arbour. At times someone else's garden or a public garden is best for this activity, as it frees me from the compulsion to be gardening, as opposed to being in the garden. I am only the most recent of those who use the garden in this way. Thomas Jefferson developed his theories of rural democracy while working the grounds of his beloved Monticello. The garden was a frequent background in the poems of Elizabeth Barrett Browning as she struggled with the themes of love, equality and gender. Henry David Thoreau made his garden and the adjacent Walden Woods famous. More recently, Canadian writer Patrick Lane chose the garden as terrain on which to confront addiction. It is a place to think about mental boundaries as well as ecological ones. My own mental parameters are perhaps a deviation or two beyond normal, whatever that is, and I see how those same mental dimensions can easily extend outward into pain and personal difficulty. I wonder just how the safe boundaries get drawn for some and erased for others. A fit subject for garden work.

Gardens are intermediaries for natural vegetation, just as dogs are windows that allow us to peer into the world of wild animals. When Spud and I dig dandelions, he knows intuitively — and perhaps genetically — that we are in a cooperative process. He can't dig dandelions out of the ground, and I don't have the agility to catch them in midair. Spud doesn't invite me to do my part, nor does he question how well I do it. He simply assumes that I *will* do my part, which is to find, sever, uproot and fling dandelions, so he can do his, which is to catch them and shred them into small bits. Like the yucca and its moth, we do make an odd pair.

As ecosystems proceed in succession, they become self-actualizing, complex, and metastable. My garden is following that trajectory, as there is less and less for me to do. Once I was the chief architect, now I am a just a bit player in a quirky domestic ecosystem, in which the human and the wild are fondly interwoven.

DON GAYTON is the author of three books of non-fiction (*The Wheatgrass Mechanism*, *Landscapes of the Interior*, *Kokanee*), and numerous technical and popular articles. His writing has won several honours, including the Canadian Science Writer's Award, the Saskatchewan Writers Guild Non-Fiction Award, and the US National Outdoor Book Award. Don has worked as a grassland specialist for both the Saskatchewan and British Columbia governments, and currently works as an ecologist for FORREX in British Columbia's Okanagan Valley.